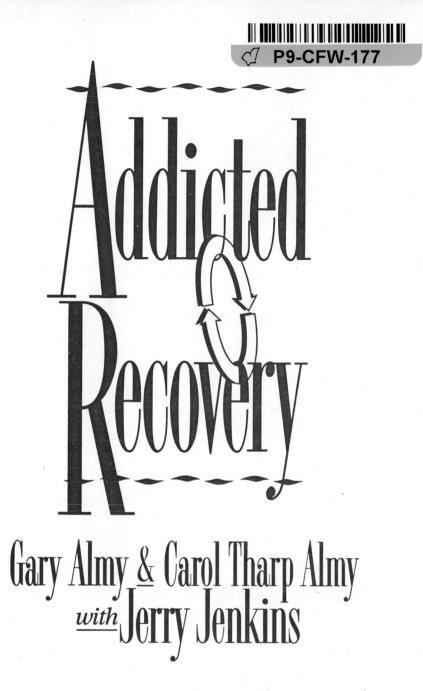

Addicted to Recovery

Gary Almy & Carol Tharp Almy
with Jerry Jenkins

Blakemore Piano Services
P.O. Box 113
Beaverton OR 97075

HARVEST HOUSE PUBLISHERS
Eugene, Oregon 97402

Names and incidental details of persons appearing in this book have been changed in order to protect the privacy of the individuals involved.

ADDICTED TO RECOVERY

Copyright © 1994 by Gary Almy, Carol Tharp Almy, and Jerry B. Jenkins
Published by Harvest House Publishers
Eugene, Oregon 97402

Library of Congress Cataloging-in-Publication Data

Almy, Gary, 1942–
    Addicted to recovery : exposing the false gospel of psychotherapy :
escaping the trap of victim mentality / Gary Almy & /Carol Tharp Almy
with Jerry Jenkins.
      p.   cm.
    ISBN 1-56507-185-9
    1. Psychiatry and religion.   2. Psychotherapy—Religious aspects—
Christianity.   3. Psychotherapy—Moral and ethical aspects.
4. Christian life. I. Almy, Carol Tharp, 1949- . II. Jenkins, Jerry B.
III. Title.
RC455.4.R4A42   1994
616.89'14—dc20   94-11489
                                                      CIP

Printed in the United States of America.

94 95 96 97 98 99 00 — 10 9 8 7 6 5 4 3 2 1

To our children, God's gift:
Julie, Matthew, Nancy, Tim, and Johnny

"You came of the Lord Adam and the Lady Eve," said Aslan. "And that is both honour enough to erect the head of the poorest beggar, and shame enough to bow the shoulder of the greatest emperor in the earth."

(From *Prince Caspian* by C.S. Lewis, copyright 1951 by Collier Books, Macmillan Publishing Co., Inc.)

Contents

1

Our Own Stories

◆————◆

WE REALIZE THAT NO MATTER how many people pick up this book, we are writing, always, to an audience of one—you. Our handicap is that we don't know why you were attracted to a book on this subject. You may feel in need of recovery. You may feel you have been burned by the recovery movement. You may have a friend or a loved one in need of counsel and you want to be able to steer them the right way and away from the wrong way.

Let us tell you at the outset, this book is a polemic. That means we come at this subject from one distinct end of the spectrum. We hold strong views and we will do our best to elucidate them here.

Many will tell you that the recovery movement has peaked or has already become passé. Don't believe it. The movement may have a different label, and perhaps some of its buzzwords may have changed, but secular and Christian publishers are still pumping out books on the subject. And recovery counseling centers abound. Frankly, we see grave dangers and appreciate the opportunity to expose them and suggest alternatives here.

Who are we and why do we care? We are Christians first, both coming to faith in Christ as adults. We are medical doctors, having met during our training. Gary is a psychiatrist and an associate chief of staff at Hines Veterans Hospital (Maywood, Illinois). He is also associate professor of psychiatry at Loyola Medical School (Chicago). Carol is a dermatologist in private practice in Winnetka, Illinois, and is also on the dermatology faculty at Northwestern University Medical School (Chicago).

It may seem ironic—due to our admitted bias against "talk" therapy in general—that we are also founders and board members of the Biblical Counseling Center (Arlington Heights, Illinois). This is a nonprofit ministry we founded five years ago in hopes of raising a standard for truth in the morass of psychotherapy passing as "Christian counseling" in the Chicago area. You'll see as we go how we distinguish between true biblical counseling and the feel-good therapy so prevalent and popular in this age of dysfunction and recovery.

You'll discover why we cannot align ourselves with Christians, however well-intentioned, who see value in integrating psychiatry and psychology with the Bible. In our opinion, psychiatry in North America is just psychology on Prozac. More importantly, we have come to see as heretical the idea that there is "new" knowledge for emotional problems "more practical" than Scripture. Those who find value in "gleaning from everything"—often that "everything" includes disciplines with humanistic, anti-God bases—are on dangerous ground.

Meanwhile, let us tell you our individual stories so you'll understand where we've come from and something of how we have arrived at our conclusions. We're not just physicians, scientists, or theoreticians. We're the parents of five adopted children. We've endured marital, financial, and kid troubles. And there were times in our history when we would have been perfect candidates for feel-good recovery treatment. Thank God we escaped that!

Carol's Story

I was born in 1942, the eldest of three daughters on a farm in southeast Iowa. My mother faithfully took us to Sunday school at the local church in Monterey. There a godly woman named Margaret Johnson taught me the great Bible stories. After hearing one of these, it came to me that I could ask God to take away my bad dream. At six years old I was waking every night from a nightmare of a lion chasing me.

The dream never came again after the night I asked God to take it away. I found that so amazing and wonderful that I told everyone the next day at my one-room country school. It clearly made many people uncomfortable, and I learned that I should keep my thoughts of God to myself.

My father, a moral man with high standards in all areas, was impressed by scientific progress and looked to the university as the hope for our future. My parents were living examples of the Protestant work ethic in action, and for that I will always be grateful.

Like so many Americans at that time, my mother was impressed by Norman Vincent Peale and his "power of positive thinking." Peale's popular little magazine, *Guideposts*, was a standard feature in our home, as was a little book from the Danforth Foundation on "building your life four-square" (physically, mentally, socially, and spiritually). As I grew older I would try the techniques offered in these publications, but the efforts always ended in frustration and discouragement.

My parents endured community criticism for enrolling me in a distant high school, which they rightfully felt would better prepare me for the university than would the community high school. I boarded the bus at 6:45 in the morning and didn't reach home until 5:30 in the evening. When I developed an aching back, I assumed it was due to those long days. However, in November of my freshman year I learned that the ache was due to a heavy tumor called a leiomyosarcoma pulling on the muscles of the lower back.

Our family doctor immediately sent me one hundred miles north to the University Hospital in Iowa City. The case appeared hopeless, but Dr. Elizabeth Coffin decided to cut all day to free my body of as much of that cancer as she could. Throughout my high school years that sarcoma continued to spread to my lungs. Another doctor, M.S. Lawrence, continued to cut, and eventually—after more abdominal procedures in my college years—the cancer disappeared. One can only imagine the directions a therapist might take an adult who's had an adolescence like that.

Framed on the wall of the house where I took piano lessons was the quote: "All things work together for good to them that love God." I did not know it was from the Bible (Romans 8:28). I had read all the books of Dr. Tom Dooley's work in Viet Nam and had decided even before I entered the hospital that I wanted to be a missionary surgeon. I had never met a missionary and had little idea what the word meant. Until I went to Iowa City for the cancer surgery I had met no one in the medical field outside our family doctor. As I lay recovering on those open wards, I loved to watch the doctors make their rounds with residents, interns, and students following. It exposed me to a world otherwise closed to a teenage farm girl.

My parents urged me, gently but firmly, away from a serious high school romance and on to the University of Iowa when I was seventeen. I see this now as coming from the loving hand of a sovereign God; at the time, however, I found it overwhelmingly painful.

I had no interest in the social life at the university. I didn't drink, I didn't smoke, and I had no interest in Big Ten football. To me the atmosphere was impersonal, godless, and without purpose. I looked for peace of mind and couldn't find it. I developed eating disorders before they were popular and had names.

I found a church of the same mainline denomination as the old Monterey church, but I found the sermons empty and meaningless. I tried to build my life "four square" as the book had taught, but it seemed futile. This was the university, where I could supposedly fulfill my plans to become a missionary doctor, but I found no pleasure in it at all.

I found my roommate's diary left open on her desk one day and read an entry about myself. She wrote that she had never seen anyone with my discipline, my study habits, and my general perfection. I saw this as confirmation of the utter emptiness in my well-ordered life. It was isolated perfectionism without meaning. Seeing the words she had written depressed me even more. She was impressed with the life of a miserable young woman. I felt numb when I was accepted into medical school the third year of college. I saw only the heaviness of the treadmill ahead.

While working a summer job in New England I met a distinguished older gentleman in Vermont who had just retired from a professorship at Union Theological Seminary in New York City. I thought I had finally found someone who could give me answers related to life and purpose. Instead he leaned against a split-rail fence with a beautiful mountain stream flowing behind him, bowed his head, and said, "I don't know if I believe anything at all. I don't know if anything I've taught all these years is true or if life has any meaning."

If the seminary professor had no answers, who did? I was nearly suicidal at this point.

I returned to Iowa City in September, started medical school, and after only two months left in existential despair. I had no words for what I felt, but in spite of that the dean of the medical school dealt with me with unusual compassion. To leave medical school is to reject a much-prized opportunity, and rarely was anyone given a second chance. He told me I could consider it a "leave of absence" and return the next year if I wanted.

I worked in a kidney research lab, moved in with two women students, found I could even laugh occasionally, and returned to medical school the next September. After another surgical procedure for the cancer, I began to tell myself, "Eat, drink, and be merry, for tomorrow you may die." I decided it would be better to have lived and lost than never to have lived at all.

At this point when I was ready to try anything, George Luiken, a classmate acquaintance, invited me to a picnic I later learned was a function of InterVarsity Christian Fellowship. There a dental student named Mark Peterson introduced himself and wasted little time asking me if I knew the Lord.

Did I know the Lord? What a strange question! I sensed Mark was sincere and serious, and I told him I had no idea what it meant to know the Lord. I had gone to church, knew some Bible stories, prayed, even memorized Scripture, and often sought God with real desperation. But did I know the Lord? Not in the least! I loved old hymns, and I asked Mark to explain the lyrics in the song "Jesus Took My Burden."

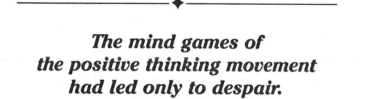

***The mind games of
the positive thinking movement
had led only to despair.***

He told me that all my attempts to live right constituted an attempt to earn my way into heaven, which he said would never happen. He told me that God's holiness and perfection were the standard and that they stood infinitely distant from my level of achievement. He told me that my works counted little more than those of the common criminal in approaching the Creator of the universe.

Many seem to find such theology an insult, but to me these were some of the most precious words I had ever heard. It was absolute truth; I had never been able to build my life "four square." The mind games of the positive thinking movement had led only to despair.

Mark showed me from the book of Romans that all have sinned and come short of the glory of God (3:23). I did not hesitate when he asked if I wanted to pray to receive God's only begotten son as atonement for my sin. John Bunyan's Pilgrim (from *Pilgrim's Progress*), when he said, "He hath given me rest by his sorrow and life by his death," could not have felt greater relief from the load than I did when "Jesus took the burden I could no longer bear."

I read the book of Romans that night from the *Living Epistles* book Mark gave me. I especially loved chapters seven and eight, because up to then I thought I was alone in crying out, "O how wretched I am! Who will deliver me from this body of death?" (7:24). Only now was I able to say with Paul, "There is no condemnation" (8:1).

That tiny InterVarsity group provided my Christian fellowship through the rest of medical school. In July of 1968 I took my *Living Bible* and C.S. Lewis's *Mere Christianity* to my internship at St. Albans Naval Hospital in New York City. With no Christian fellowship and not knowing where to seek it, I should have read again Romans 6 where Paul answers his question, "What shall we say then? Shall we go on sinning so that grace may increase?" I was all too close to that kind of thinking about my freedom in Christ at that time.

It was during that period that I met and began dating Gary.

Gary's Story

I led a seemingly trouble-free childhood, giving little thought to any deeper things in life. I grew up in a nominal Christian home in Omaha, Nebraska, went to a mainline denominational church, and said the same prayer before supper every evening. I remember no discussion of spiritual things, and religious life or thoughts didn't touch me.

I had no value system that took into consideration either God or other people. I fancied a materialistic lifestyle and can see now that without being obviously ill-mannered about it, I was consumed with self. My life was empty, but unlike Carol I was not aware of it. I had no convictions about anything and was surely an uninteresting personality.

I rotated through the various clinical service areas in medical school at the University of Nebraska, as does every student, and became fascinated with psychiatry. The faculty seemed to be the nicest, they were admired by their patients, and they even had senses of humor. Psychiatry appeared to be a pleasant place to rest after the hard work of medical school.

I began to read all the psychoanalytic literature I could find, and the pursuit became religious. Here was a so-called medical discipline that claimed to have the answers to life! Who are we? Why are we here? What makes us do what we do? The "secret knowledge" of the psychiatric community was opening to me, and I found it immensely attractive. I felt proud to be one of the elite admitted to its "wisdom." I did not recognize the circular reasoning, nor did I question the scientific validity. Wasn't it an established part of the medical community? Why should I question it?

C.S. Lewis wrote in 1947 in *The Abolition of Man:* "The serious magical endeavor and the serious scientific endeavor are twins... born of the same impulse. For the wise men of old, the cardinal problem has been how to conform the soul to reality... For magic and applied science alike, the problem is how to subdue reality to the wishes of men. The solution is a technique." I had never heard of C.S. Lewis. Never had I thought of the techniques of psychoanalysis from that perspective.

Carol and I left New York City in July of 1969. She went west to begin dermatology training at the University of California in San Francisco. I went east, as I owed the Navy one year of general medical duty, and was assigned to a supply ship in the Mediterranean. The old adage that absence makes the heart grow fonder proved true for us that year, and we were wed in 1970.

I began psychiatric residency at the Naval Hospital in Oakland, California, and there met Dr. Michael Taylor. He was a Jewish man from New York City and was my first supervisor in the residency. No Bible-belt fundamentalist could have felt stronger about the errors of psychiatry than did Dr. Taylor. Like me, he had entered the field with the goal of becoming a psychoanalyst. After two years of analysis in New York City, it would be an understatement to say he lost respect for the field. He viewed psychotherapy as a waste of time, illogical, unscientific, and wrong. Mickey was an engaging, convincing teacher. I could not deny his conclusions.

The longer I worked with Dr. Taylor, the more ridiculous my previous plans seemed. Psychiatry had been for me the path of least resistance, aside from becoming a religious pursuit. I had envisioned myself sitting for fifty minutes, listening to a patient willing to pay large sums for me to wax eloquent on Freud's theories. How dull that looked now! Watching Mickey work with patients was as exciting as watching successful surgery. He took Viet Nam vets who entered the hospital truly insane, hearing voices, high on drugs, and genuinely psychotic, examined them, studied their lab reports, prescribed medication, monitored them, and sent them back to duty with minds cleared. I stood amazed and changed my direction toward "biological psychiatry."

Mickey practiced neurology applied to behavior. He stressed that we should be interested only in that research that was truly scientifically measurable. He taught us to focus on the chemistry of the brain and the influence of structural abnormalities of that brain on the patient's behavior.

Spiritual problems were never mentioned, and I had no concept of such. If the problem could not be proven to be biological, I assumed the patient was emotionally weak. I laughingly told students, "You don't really have to talk to these patients; just medicate them." Carol has since said that with no more than I had to offer, it was a blessing I *didn't* talk to the patients.

Carol:

Science and the universities still seemed to me to be filled with people functioning like unfeeling robots, and psychiatry seemed to attract people who wanted more than that from life. I assumed in those days that

the theories of psychiatry-psychology-psychoanaly-
sis could be blended with the good news of the Messiah that had set me free. I foolishly thought I had
found it all: the comfort and security of the believer,
along with the respect of the world via medicine and
psychiatry.

But one morning I read in one of Gary's psychiatric
journals a study that showed the highest suicide rate
of all medical professionals was among psychiatrists
and women physicians. Shaken, I tried to forget about
it. Then Gary's best friend from medical school, who
had started a psychiatric residency, lost his wife to a
self-inflicted gunshot to the head. Then one of Gary's
favorite professors of psychiatry killed himself with no
warning to anyone. Then the wife of a friend who was
an expert on depression killed herself.

Gary:

These suicides upset Carol terribly. She told me,
"They would not have done it if they had known their
Savior." She talked more and more like that. Though I
too was shocked by these deaths, I chose not to deal
with it.

Carol had discovered J. Vernon McGee's "Through
the Bible" program on her car radio one morning, and
he quickly became a favorite. She kept listening and
recounting to me at dinner what she had heard each
day. She wasn't overbearing and seemed to make no
demands of me, so I just accepted it as one more evidence of our disparate personalities. She could get
intense about things; I prided myself in being laid back
and controlled. I even tagged along when she sang in
the choral concerts at Old First Church in San Francisco.

We lived an idyllic life in California. Our specialties gave us unusually reasonable work hours for residents in training. After hours we went to restaurants and movies, socialized with other residents, and traveled. When the Navy assigned me to Great Lakes Naval Hospital north of Chicago for two years, we assumed we would return to San Francisco after that, as Carol had a dermatology practice waiting for her there.

Carol:

I wanted to adopt children. If I was never to be a medical missionary, I could at least reach out to some "less adoptable" infants—the physically handicapped and/or racially mixed. Gary agreed. The babies came rather quickly and easily and became challenges as well as joys. We were hardly prepared for such challenges and could not have predicted them. Our classic yuppie life soon faded. By the time the third baby arrived in four years, our marriage, our finances, and our stability were precarious. Thoughts of returning to San Francisco were gone. I had a private dermatology practice with its usual demands, a four-year-old son, a two-year-old daughter, and a newborn who hardly ever slept and seemed to never stop crying. In addition, I had a neglected husband who wouldn't stop spending money.

Gary and I began fighting over everything. I was exhausted and any feeling of love we had had was completely gone. Gary started me on an antidepressant medication, but I was too tired to remember to take it. I developed a rash from it anyway and gave it up after only a few days.

I went from church to church looking for one that would teach the Bible. I had still not ventured beyond the mainline denominations, fearing I might get caught up in some cult. I was desperate enough to follow a flier in the mailbox to a new church meeting in the basement of a local junior high school. The word "evangelical" frightened me, and I entered cautiously, sitting alone in the back.

When the church holds the diamonds of Scripture in its hands, why does it go elsewhere for counsel?

A thin, little man taught from Haggai. I had not known that book was in the Bible, and though I had never heard of Haggai, I knew now that he was speaking to me. "Give careful thought to your ways. You have planted much, but have harvested little. You eat, but never have enough. You drink, but never have your fill. You put on clothes, but are not warm. You earn wages, only to put them in a purse with holes in it" (Haggai 1:5-6).

How much Gary and I needed to hear that warning! We were caught in a maze of money, education, big homes, youth, Ferraris and Cadillacs, everything the world had to offer. "Meaningless! Meaningless!" says the teacher. "Utterly meaningless! Everything is meaningless" (Ecclesiastes 1:1-2).

As this church grew, a full-time pastor came. I finally went to him and pleaded for help. Dr. Paul

Engle, who later became our dear friend, handled our problems with great wisdom. He phoned Gary, saying he would like to meet with us Saturday mornings for marital counseling. I was stunned! He was going to do this regularly at no charge!

Gary:

Carol had encouraged me to try this church with her a few times. I knew I needed something, so I did not greatly resist. I saw something there I had never seen before: the Bible clearly taught, and seemingly normal people living the Christian life and shamelessly talking about it. Several there had Ph.D.s. I was shocked. I had always assumed that education made one recognize that Scripture was not to be taken seriously.

Dr. and Mrs. David Hesselgrave, a local seminary professor and his wife who were members of the church, even visited our home. They exhibited the love of Christ in such a way that I was astounded. The people of the church even brought meals to us when Carol was hospitalized with pneumonia. I had never known people like this.

Pastor Engle visited our home every week and counseled us from Scripture. Previously I would have resented this as an invasion of my privacy, but I was by this time aware that nothing in my life was working. Having material possessions, playing the all-knowing psychiatrist, being promoted to chief of the psychiatric service at the hospital—none of it was bringing relief. And now here came this man with answers from the Book! He assigned homework and encouraged us to have daily time together in prayer and Scripture.

Carol:

I felt then that I hated my husband. I did what Pastor Engle suggested, only because I knew God expected it of me. Dr. Engle had told me clearly, though with compassion and understanding, that I did not have Scriptural cause to exit my marriage. Without enthusiasm I read the books we were given and I prayed and read the Bible with Gary as instructed. I reminded myself that this was not the first time in my life I had said with Peter, "Lord, to whom shall we go? You have the words of eternal life" (John 6:7).

Among other life-changing things we learned were these truths (jarring to two who had been so enamored with the counsel of the world): "And He [the Messiah] will be called Wonderful Counselor" (Isaiah 9:6). "When he comes, he will convict the world of guilt in regard to sin and righteousness and judgment" (John 16:8).

It was wonderful to recognize guilt as real, rather than as a disabling emotion. With that reality came answers. Guilt is real, and we are guilty. Judgment is real; we live in a moral universe. How desperately mankind needs that atonement that God provided! I stood amazed at a pastor who would help us and was not intimidated by a psychiatrist. Even more amazing was that Gary was submitting to it.

Gary:

I was going along and doing as I was told, thinking that if I gave it enough time, certainly something good would happen. There came a point when I went to Paul Engle in tears with things at their lowest ebb again, and it was then that I received Christ. I finally knew that I could do nothing to even help myself, much less save myself.

We've now been at it for years, trying to face sins, accepting personal responsibility for them, repenting, growing together in the Lord, and applying His Word to all of life. We have even adopted two more children.

As we have grown in Christ we have had to ask ourselves, when the church holds the diamonds of Scripture in its hands, why does it go elsewhere for counsel? Why is the church so fascinated with the polluted crumbs that fall upon it from Freud's table?

We hope in this book to give you facts about Gary's medical specialty, to warn you of the pitfalls of psychotherapy, to show you that it presents a false gospel and a false view of mankind, and to thus help you escape the trap of victim mentality that permeates our society.

2

The Problem with Jennie
PART ONE

✦———————✦

O<small>UR EXAMPLES AND CASE STUDIES</small> come from personal encounters with real people. All names and incidental details have been changed to protect identities. Some of the stories are composites, but all pertinent facts are true and documented. You may find some of our stories incredible, but we assure you we have left out literally hundreds of accounts with which we are personally connected and which are even more bizarre.

Scripture clearly teaches that we are sinners, depraved and separated from God. We need atonement and redemption. But the church and many of its counselors have been swept along with the trend toward a victim-based society. If we can blame our problems on something from our past, we have little or no responsibility.

Let us make clear that we do not assume that all accounts of childhood trauma are false. Nor do we believe that clients who have false memories intentionally set out to destroy reputations and lives. They come to really believe these memories have been repressed.

We must also clarify that not all parents who have been accused are innocent. But there are clear Scriptural and legal guidelines to follow when making serious allegations, and even guilty parties deserve due process.

Consider, then, the story of a woman we'll call Jennie. While we have camouflaged and adjusted enough details to protect her identity, her story is wholly true.

Jennie is 32 years old, married, and the mother of two elementary school children. Her husband, Phil, is in middle management. The couple are churchgoing Christians who have agreed that Jennie should work only part time when the children are at school. She's also a volunteer at church and is involved in a women's Bible study. She and Phil were raised in Christian homes and seem, to all outward appearances, to have a happy home life.

However, Jennie has recently begun noticing the stirrings of persistent moodiness, vague resentment, mounting intolerance of stress. She's short-tempered with Phil and the children, and she realizes this has been going on long enough that she can't attribute it all to premenstrual syndrome.

When she finds herself having difficulty falling asleep and staying asleep, often waking at four or five in the morning and staring at the ceiling for hours, she realizes she's depressed. Maddeningly, she can't get a handle on what might be wrong.

Oh, there are things that bother her. She's not happy about her extra few pounds. She's irritated that Phil is often away from home on business trips and then involved in playing and watching sports when she thinks he should spend more time with the family.

But, she tells herself, these are common, modern complaints. He's otherwise loving and attentive. He has no bad habits and she has no reason to doubt his faithfulness. When she compares him with other men in her orbit, she's still happy with her choice. Phil may not be the pillar of the church her father was, but how many men are?

He has learned to placate her when she's irritable, and he rarely snaps back at her when she's "in a mood." But they both feel she has a problem. She's decided that she's depressed for some reason, and Phil can't deny that she has the symptoms. He asks what more she could want out of life. She tearfully admits she doesn't know.

Finally, one Sunday morning after church, they approach their pastor. "We need marital counseling," they tell him.

"Really? What's going on?"

Jennie admits her feelings, and the pastor, apparently wishing for more specific complaints, says he feels what they are looking for is beyond his level of expertise. "Why don't I refer you to Douglas Miller? He's a counseling psychologist, you know."

They knew. Jennie and Phil had long admired Dr. Miller, who was a longtime church leader. They set an appointment.

The first meeting is cordial but awkward. Phil's view is that he and his wife agree she has a problem and they're wondering if Dr. Miller can help. The counselor asks a lot of questions, gets the history of their relationship, and sends them away with some assignments.

They are to talk to each other several minutes a day, get personal, reach beneath the surface, schedule a date each week, touch each other more. Phil is to negotiate for his time away from the family and try to cut back on that by one outing each week.

Understandably to both husband and wife, the bulk of the work falls on her. She is to carefully examine herself after each outburst, look within herself for motives, slights, hurts, reasons. She is to speak her mind to Phil if he offends her.

Jennie came away from the appointment cautiously hopeful. It nagged at her that though there was a picture of Jesus on the wall of Dr. Miller's office and that she saw a Bible on the credenza behind his desk, he neither prayed nor referred to Scripture. He mentioned the Lord a few times, expressed confidence that God cared, and reminded her that their testimony would be affected by the progress they made. That made sense to her.

That night she slept better than she had in weeks, and for the next three days she was more patient. She awoke before dawn the following morning, however, and felt despondent. She searched her soul for a reason and realized she had been nice to her family only because she felt accountable to Dr. Miller. She would have to report any outbursts or failures.

She decided that was not all bad. Whatever it took to keep peace in the home was all right with her. But she had wanted to change from the inside. She had enough reasons to be a nice, well-behaved Christian wife and mother. Shouldn't living for God be enough reason to do the right things?

The day before their next appointment with the counselor, Jennie reminded Phil that he had been gone

twice without her really having a say in either decision. He told her she wasn't supposed to have a say,
but that he was supposed to cut back a bit. "I could
have been gone three times, but I wasn't."

She found herself growing angry, and she expressed
that without sarcasm or shouting, the way Dr. Miller
had recommended. "I want to feel I have some say in
your life," she said. "I'm feeling left out, and it bothers
me when I think you're neglecting the kids..."

"You mean neglecting you," Phil said, irritated.

"And me," she admitted.

"That's really it," he pushed. "You're jealous of my
time and you try to make me feel guilty about neglecting the kids."

"No, I'm—"

"You can't lay that on me," he said. "I'm with them
more than most fathers, and I put them to bed every
night."

She wanted to scream at him. She felt cornered.
She had not intended this to be an argument but rather
a healthy discussion. Fighting for control, Jennie said
just that. Phil pursed his lips and shook his head.

"And that look makes me feel like a child," she said.
"You're my husband, not my parent."

He reacted with sarcasm. "Thank the Lord for
that," he said. And she exploded. Jennie threw dishes
into the sink, wouldn't look at him when he spoke, left
the room, and slammed the door. He called out, "Here
we go again," she yelled back, "Don't start with me,"
and they went to bed not speaking.

She hardly slept.

She didn't know whether to look forward to or to
dread the appointment the next day. Phil had not
apologized, and she remembered that he seldom did.

But he had acted nicer in the morning and pretended that nothing had happened. She took that to mean he was expressing forgiveness, not sorrow, and she hated herself for appreciating it.

---◆---

> *Look what I've done to my poor husband,* **she thought.** *My depression is making me crazy and pushing him away.*

"So," Phil said, as they pulled into the parking lot of the counselor's office, "what are we going to tell him?"

"About last night?"

"Uh-huh."

"The truth."

"Which is?"

"That I lost it again."

He nodded. That irritated her.

In a small, frightened voice she said, "You know, I think you could share the blame a little on that. I thought it was just as much your fault."

He was clearly angry. "How can you say that? You drag me to this counselor, he tells you how to fix your problem, you fail, and now you want to blame me?"

She tried to argue that that's not what she was getting at, but he was already out of the car. Jennie thought about waiting to see if he would open her

door, but she knew she would be embarrassed if anyone saw her sitting there while her husband charged
on ahead. *Look what I've done to my poor husband,*
she thought. *My depression is making me crazy and
pushing him away.*

When Dr. Miller asked for a progress report, Jennie
started to tell him that the first few days had gone well,
but before she could get to the unraveling, Phil said,
"Frankly, so far this is not working." They outlined the
trouble.

Dr. Miller had a few new suggestions, some of
which seemed helpful, and for the next three weeks
Jennie felt they had made some progress. Phil, however, didn't. They weren't as confrontive with each
other as the counselor wanted, so it was always a
surprise when Phil reminded her—in front of Dr.
Miller—how many times she had reverted to her old
ways that week. She *was* aware, however, that her
sleeping patterns had not improved.

Fatigue and frustration made things worse, something the counselor had predicted. "It may get darker
before the dawn," he said cryptically. Before long that
prophecy fulfilled itself when Jennie lost interest in
the homework assignments and quit trying to avoid
venting her anger.

Finally Phil told Dr. Miller that they had better try
something more aggressive. "Did you have something
specific in mind?" the counselor asked.

"No. All I know is, this has been a waste of time. I
don't blame you, but Jennie's still the same."

"I do have a few ideas," Dr. Miller said. "If you don't
mind, I'd like to meet with Jennie alone for a few
weeks."

"That's fine with me," Phil said, "as long as it
doesn't turn into husband-bashing sessions."

Jennie was hurt by that, but the counselor took it in stride. "I can assure you I would not allow that to happen," he said. Jennie felt like a child.

The next week Jennie went alone. Dr. Miller was the perfect gentleman, leaving the office door open with his secretary outside so there would be no hint of impropriety. And he quickly changed from the condescending tone with which he had promised Phil that he wouldn't let Jennie bad-mouth her husband. Now he was an encourager. He expressed concern for her continuing depression and suggested, "Frankly, I was beginning to get the impression that we may need to explore some areas that you might not want to expose to Phil just yet. Am I right?"

Jennie, who by now was as frustrated as Phil at her lack of progress, was strangely encouraged by this change of direction. "I don't know," she said. "Maybe." She felt run down, irritable, exhausted. She was not aware of anything she didn't want Phil to know about, but the very suggestion made Dr. Miller seem like her compatriot. If there were things lurking in her mind that needed to be dealt with, he would know how to expose them and deal with them.

"I need to know," the counselor said, "that you are getting serious about turning your life around."

"I don't know about serious, but I'm desperate."

He smiled. "That's serious enough. If you're willing to really let go and relax and suspend some of your inhibitions against your anger, I think we can make some progress."

"I need to make progress," she admitted. "But what do you mean about suspending inhibitions? I certainly haven't been inhibited about showing my anger."

"I mean that in a good way, of course. I was raised the same way you were, Jennie. In the church. You've been flying off the handle and feeling guilty and depressed about it. That tells me that you may be hiding from yourself the real reasons behind your anger. Wouldn't you agree that your outbursts seem like overreactions to typical marital squabbles?"

For the first time, a light went on in Jennie's head. *Yes!* she thought. *That's true!* "In other words," she said, relieved, "it's okay to get angry, but it's not okay to lose control."

Dr. Miller said, "Not so fast. I want you to feel free even to lose control so we can really get at the root of this. If you're overreacting, then Phil is not the problem. He may be the typically insensitive husband. If you agree that doesn't justify the depression and the irritability, then we have to probe deeper."

She nodded, starting to understand but having no idea where it might lead.

"Are you willing?" he asked.

"I guess, but I don't know what you're looking for."

"Neither do I. That's why you have to help."

Jennie began feeling hope for the first time since the first session. She expressed her willingness to work with Dr. Miller, with whom she was beginning to feel more comfortable.

He probed her history with Phil, reminding her that this was all confidential, that she could tell him anything, and that she should vent her anger and frustration whenever necessary. She found herself crying at times, speaking in disgust at others, remembering all the pain of their marriage. Every time she would catch herself and say, "But, of course, it's not that bad; he's never been abusive, just insensitive," Dr. Miller would urge her to just roll with the anger.

"We're not saying Phil is a bad guy," he said. "We're just trying to see what your life with him has done to your psyche, your sense of self-worth."

What a window opened with that comment! Her self-worth! When was the last time she had felt good about herself? It had been during their courtship and early married life. Phil had been head-over-heels in love with her and showed it. Then, when the first child came along, maybe he felt neglected or maybe he felt the pressure of a new life for whom he was now also responsible. He became a little less attentive, a little more selfish and demanding, a little less loving. He found interests outside the home, and the marriage became less romantic.

Jennie admitted she felt less attractive and more harried. She wanted to be a cherished wife, the perfect mother and companion. But she was "just a house-wife." When the other baby arrived two years later, she felt trapped. All the work seemed to fall to her, and while she and Phil got out occasionally and she loved her children dearly, she had fallen into a typical early-motherhood doldrum.

After a few weeks of probing this pain, Dr. Miller had come to a conclusion. "Try this on for size," he suggested. "Tell me if I'm off base." He said that because of her upbringing and her belief in the traditional role of a Christian woman, she had allowed herself to go further than submitting herself to her husband, as the Scriptures instructed. "You didn't just submit yourself. You let him subject you. Understand?"

"Not really," she said, feeling guilty that Phil was now the villain.

"I'm not blaming Phil," the counselor said. "This remains your problem. You allowed this to happen.

Your sense of self-worth is at an all-time low, and that has made you less attractive to your husband. When he puts you in subjection, it's convenient, but your allowing it also causes him to lose respect for you."

She nodded. "I *don't* feel respected."

"You're not," Dr. Miller said. "Especially not by yourself."

"And I've tried to strike out in anger, and that doesn't work either."

He smiled. "Now we're getting somewhere. When was the last time you did something for Jennie?"

"I'm sorry?"

"When was the last time you did something for yourself, something positive? I'm not talking about attacking or defending. I'm talking about treating yourself with respect."

Jennie was silent. She couldn't remember when.

"It's time to look after yourself," Dr. Miller said. "That is my prescription. Go shopping, go to the beauty shop, read some books. Get to know and like and respect yourself again."

"But when Phil is playing golf or going to a game with his friends, I have the kids."

"Get a babysitter. We're taking care of Jennie now. When you learn to respect and like yourself, Phil will come around too."

To Jennie it was as if she had come out of the desert and now stood under a waterfall of refreshing spring water. For the next month she did just what the counselor had suggested. She felt alive again, young again, a person again. She had her own schedule and she was active and busy, sleeping better, and more assertive at home.

At first Phil was stunned and pleased. He liked the new Jennie. She seemed more at peace. Once he even called Dr. Miller to thank him for whatever he had said or done. "Thanks for giving me my old wife back," he said.

But it wasn't long before both Phil and the children began resenting the time they lost with Jennie. She was so busy and active in her own pursuits that they felt neglected. Jennie was devastated that the temporary truce was gone and that the new lifestyle had not cured the marriage. But she wasn't about to give up her new freedom. Soon she enjoyed the good part of the new life (more time for Jennie) and suffered from the old bickering at home.

◆

> *She also admitted, in her now freer state of mind— having cast off the inhibitions ... that things were, if anything, even worse at home.*

It didn't depress her like before until her anger and resentment carried over into her part-time job. Her boss was giving her a hard time. He wasn't even as understanding as Phil about her needing some time for herself. He said that if she couldn't work regular hours, he would have to find someone who could. He felt he had already bent enough to allow her to work only during school hours.

That tension spilled out in one of Jennie's sessions with Dr. Miller. She also admitted, in her now freer state of mind—having cast off the inhibitions her church upbringing had saddled her with—that things were, if anything, even worse at home.

The smile that had been playing at the corners of Dr. Miller's mouth for weeks began to fade. Jennie had sensed she was one of his star clients. What he had suggested had opened new vistas for her, and he seemed more interested and eager to see her and work with her when things were going well. When his suggestions no longer worked, it seemed to bother him.

She wanted to succeed, for his sake as well as hers. She was committed to being a good client. "What's going wrong?" she asked.

"Well," he said, "frankly I'm becoming concerned about something I'm detecting in your relationships. Think about this. The two major relationship problems in your life are between you and your husband and you and your male boss. Does that tell you anything?"

"Are you suggesting that I have a problem with—"

He interrupted. "I'm not suggesting anything. I'm asking."

"But you're saying that I—"

He held up a hand. "I want you to come to this on your own. I don't want to plant a problem in your mind."

But, Jennie thought, that was *precisely* what he had done. And maybe he was right. "Do I have a problem with authority?" He smiled. She had guessed right. She was a good client, a willing patient again. "But I don't feel as if I do," she said, her brow knitted in thought.

"I can only react to what I observe," he said. "What do you think?"

_____

"Maybe I do," she said. "Maybe I do. But why?"

"You tell me."

"I don't know."

"Have you had problems with authority in the past? With teachers? A pastor? A boss? Your parents?"

She thought long and hard. "Nothing that ever came to anything."

"Run with it, Jennie. What are you thinking?"

"Well, there were times in high school and junior college that I thought my teachers or the administration were stupid or shortsighted or something, but I could never do anything about it. I just accepted it."

"Why?"

"I just wasn't that assertive."

"Why are you assertive now?"

"You're helping me to be."

"Any other problems with authority?"

She shook her head, deep in thought. "Not that I recall."

He perked up and leaned forward. "What about something you don't recall?"

She shot him a glance. "What do you mean? If I don't remember—"

"*If* you remembered, what would it be?"

She shrugged, assuming he knew where he was going.

"Let me say this much," he said. "Often a person's problems with authority figures stem from his or her relationship with parents. Of course I'm not suggesting anything. I don't know your par—"

"Oh," she waved him off, "there's nothing there. My parents are saints. My father was the greatest dad—still is—and grandfather. I just love him."

Dr. Miller sat there seeming to smile smugly at her.

"What?" she said.

"Is there something here?"

"Like what?"

"I'm just saying, you're idealizing. Your father may be a wonderful man, but we both know no one is really a saint. You're not implying he's perfect—"

"Oh, no, of course not. I'm just saying he's one of the most admired men in my home church and community. Everybody thinks he's the greatest, and so do I."

"Thinks?"

"Yes, well, knows!"

"You're aware that you said they *think* he's the greatest. That means they could be wrong?"

She shook her head, not liking this. "I just meant they think it, that's how they see him and consider him."

"But how about you?"

"I see him the same way. We're barking up the wrong tree now."

"Are you being a little defensive here?"

Jennie felt her anger rising. She sensed that Dr. Miller was leading her and directing her thoughts in ways she thought inappropriate for a Christian. She wasn't going to put up with this. "Now look here," she began, quickly realizing that she was shouting and beginning to cry. She stopped herself and glanced out the door at the secretary, who quickly averted her eyes.

"No, please," Dr. Miller said, "go with this. This is good. Don't inhibit your true feelings."

She spoke forcefully in a sobbing whisper. "My father is as close to a perfect person as I have ever met. I've always loved him and been proud that he's my dad, and that's all there is to it."

_____

"Why does this upset you so?"

"Because you're implying—"

"No, no, no, don't misunderstand me, Jennie. I'm trying to help you, that's all. Don't you see that if there was any reason for you to resent your father, you're not allowing yourself to vent it? It comes out against your husband, your boss, and [he paused for effect] even your therapist."

She tried to smile, upset at herself. *Why does this bother me?* she wondered. *Why do I have my dad on such a pedestal?*

"You know," he continued, "you may be right. There may be nothing here. But I would feel better about you and your self-esteem if you were able to have a loving relationship with your father that was more realistic, more down to earth, a relationship that allowed him to be human."

That made sense. She'd have to think about that.

"Again," he said, standing to indicate the end of their session, "I'm not implying or suggesting anything. But it has been my experience, and there is a lot of clinical evidence to support this, that occasionally—not always—it comes out that an idealized view of a parent is the result of the repressing of bad memories."

"Of what?"

"Oh, it varies. It could be anything. In your case, since you do not seem to allow yourself to see your father as an imperfect human being, you could be repressing any memory of him acting in a way that conflicts with your image of him."

Jennie was so deep in thought that she realized she was squinting. "He *is* wonderful," she said simply. "Did you ever think of that? What if he just is what he appears to be?"

"Then you'd be the luckiest daughter on the face of the earth," Dr. Miller said. "Out of all the kids alive, you're the one who got the perfect parent."

Jennie tried to detect any hint of sarcasm. Her therapist was smiling. "But then why do I have a problem with self-esteem and with authority?"

"Precisely," he said, looking at his watch. "I have an appointment waiting."

Jennie felt rushed, but she didn't want to leave him this way. It was too unsettling. "What should I be doing about this?"

"Well, if you're so certain I'm off base, then nothing."

"No, I'm willing to think about it. You're making some sense."

"Thanks."

"I didn't mean it that way."

"I know. Just do me a favor before next time. Rack your brain. Relax and let yourself really think about this, again allowing yourself to loosen your normal inhibition about thinking negatively about your father. And just try to remember a time or two when he wasn't a saint."

She scowled.

"It doesn't have to be anything bad or serious," he said. "Just one time when he was unfair to you or raised his voice or was unreasonable. Even if that's all you come up with and we decide he's not the root of your authority problem, this will be a healthy exercise."

"I'll try," she said.

And she did.

3

The Problem with Jennie

PART TWO

The Pseudo-memory Pandemic

◆———————◆

FOR THE NEXT FEW WEEKS, Jennie tried to fight the idea that her father was anything less than she had always thought. However, her behavior at home and at her part-time job seemed still to evidence what Dr. Miller had called her "authority problem." He continued to remind her that "father problems" were common, and even provided her with a list of trauma effects."[1] Dr. Miller told Jennie that several studies had shown adult problems to be related to repressed memories of early abuse and that she need not feel alone in this.

Enough of the "evidences of trauma" coincided with Jennie's own failure and frustrations that she came to believe she surely needed to work harder to remember her "real" relationship with her father. Dr. Miller said she could still be in denial and still repressing some childhood rift.

For a few days Jennie gave herself time to sit and reminisce about her father. At first all she could remember were happy times. He had been so loving and supportive, and so loyal. He always encouraged her and bragged about her. He was strict, sure, but she had needed that in school. It resulted in good grades, and she had felt motivated but not obsessed.

Had he ever hurt her? Maybe that time when she was about four and he hollered at her in front of one of her friends. He had yelled at her before, but this time she was innocent. She tried to defend herself and he threatened to send her friend home. When she pouted he ordered her to her room where he gave her a stern lecture and warned her again that she would be spanked if she didn't straighten up.

As she recalled this incident, she seemed to relive it. She didn't like her daddy this way. His being cross with her hadn't bothered her when she had been caught doing something wrong, because she felt she deserved it. But his being wrong about a situation was new to her. She had learned that he wasn't perfect, that he could be human and make a mistake. And she couldn't fix it.

So this was what repression was! She hadn't thought about that for years! Was there more? Had he said or done something inappropriate, or had he simply been wrong once? If he was wrong once, could he have been wrong other times? She forced herself to dredge up a few more times, once when he was cross with her mother and another time when he demanded they watch the TV program he wanted to watch, even though the entire rest of the family preferred something else.

Jennie hated thinking like this, but perhaps it was healthier. Then she remembered that during an angry moment with her dad when she was in high school she wondered what everyone at church would think if they heard him raising his voice. Now she remembered that she had even suggested that to him.

◆

At their next session, her counselor reminded her that her problems were not going away because she had not delved deeply enough to get at the root causes.

He appeared embarrassed and defensive, and he had laughed at her. That made her mad. He said, "You think the pastor doesn't lose his temper once in a while?"

She had said something nasty, like, "Not the way you do," to which he had replied, "If he had my family he might."

She had left the room and slammed the door. The memory was so similar to the kind of confrontations and results she had been having with Phil that it rocked her. She could take thinking this way about her father for only so long and she quickly busied herself with other things.

But soon she could think of little else. Was it possible Dr. Miller was right? Was her father not all he was cracked up to be? Of course these incidents had been minor, normal, and even fewer in number than most children have to deal with. But hadn't she repressed them? Why? And what else might she be repressing?

At their next session, her counselor reminded her that her problems were not going away because she had not delved deeply enough to get at the root causes. When she reported on her time of reflection and what she had been able to remember, he seemed to come alive.

She noticed even Dr. Miller's body language was different. He leaned forward, all eyes and ears. "You see?" he said. "You had him idealized. We need to know why."

"But these incidents weren't all that bad. I think I dealt with them by realizing that he could be wrong. I had been more unreasonable than that and nobody disowned *me.* I could give him a little slack."

"So that's what you've been doing for the last fifteen years? Cutting him a little slack by turning him into a saint?"

She shrugged. "I guess. You think I'm repressing something?"

"I didn't say that; you did."

She couldn't argue that point. But when she failed to come up with any more bad memories of her father, Dr. Miller settled back in his chair and seemed resigned to the fact that she either was not trying or was boring. She so desperately wanted to be a good client and to get past these problems in her life.

At their next session she sat on a question for nearly the first half-hour. Finally, when they seemed to have covered the same ground over and over, she broached the subject. "Dr. Miller, are dreams significant?"

"They certainly can be," he said, sitting up. "The subconscious mind often deals with things we are afraid to think about consciously."

"Well, I had a dream this week, my first nightmare since I was a child."

Now she had his full attention. "Tell me about it."

"I felt as if I were suffocating. A large dark object settled over me and covered me. I couldn't breathe. It was so huge and ominous that I was petrified. I struggled but could make no noise and could hardly move. The effort woke me up and I was nearly hyperventilating. My heart was racing. I was amazed that Phil slept through it."

"Did you tell him about it?"

"No. I didn't know what to make of it. Should I tell him?"

"Only if it will help you sort it out."

"I don't think he needs to know that I have yet another problem. He's getting pretty impatient with this counseling since I'm not getting better."

"Do you feel these sessions have not been helpful?"

"Oh, no, I appreciate them and look forward to them, though they are not always comfortable. I feel better being able to tell you everything, but I have to admit I'm still depressed and irritable and having a problem with authority."

"What do you make of the dream, Jennie?"

"I was going to ask you that. I have no idea."

"None?"

She shook her head, assuming he was about to tell her.

Instead, he had her tell and retell the dream, carefully asking questions. "Is the object a person? A man?

Did you see a face? What did you smell? What did you hear?" They didn't get far, because the dream would not come any clearer to her than it had originally. When she left she sensed he had been excited that they were potentially onto something, yet disappointed that she didn't come up with more detail.

That week she thought about the dream and Dr. Miller and the fact that she had not discussed it with Phil. She felt as if her life was unraveling. She was close to losing her job, and two of her arguments with Phil resulted in his saying things she didn't want to hear. He didn't suggest a separation, but for the first time he seemed to be giving up. "I don't know what I'm supposed to do or say!" he would rage. "This doesn't make sense anymore."

What didn't make sense? What she said? Herself? The marriage? Life? What? She was sure she didn't want to know. What she needed and wanted was for him to embrace her, to tell her that he was still behind her, that he loved her and believed in her and that he knew she would get better.

She had given up hope that he would take any responsibility for the rough waters they were going through. He had long since abandoned his part of the agreement to cut down on his time away from home. She always knew where he was and whom he was with and what he was doing, but still she felt neglected when she needed him most. When she challenged him on it, he said he was no longer in counseling, was not accountable to Dr. Miller, and that his temporary cutback had not improved things. "Sometimes I think we do better when we're not together constantly. I appreciate you more."

That cut through her soul. He was still interested in a sexual relationship with her, but it hurt her that those were the only times when he was physically affectionate. She did her best to accede to his wishes because she worried that physical love was the only thing holding him. She did not enjoy it, however, because she felt distant from him and resented his emotional desertion. She tried her best to hide that, because he became irritable and insulted if he detected lack of interest on her part.

One night after they had made love—despite typical comments by him earlier in the evening, such as the above—she bolted awake at two in the morning, soaked with sweat. The dream had returned and this time it was worse. She had struggled so long that she feared she would die under the weight pressing down on her. She sobbed until she could catch her breath and her pulse steadied. Phil awoke and asked what was the matter.

She took a deep breath. "I just had a bad dream," she said.

"Oh, that's good. You okay now?"

"Yeah."

He rolled over and was immediately asleep. She didn't know what to think. Part of her was strangely moved by his almost compassionate question whether she was okay. Another part of her hated herself for having downplayed the terror by saying it was "just" a bad dream. It had been a horrible nightmare, worse than the first, something she never wanted to experience again. She wondered if she would ever look forward to sleeping again.

Two nights later she was just drifting off when the feeling of terror overcame her. Before she saw or felt or experienced anything, she forced herself awake and lay there all night, fighting sleep. With nothing else to do, even though she didn't want to think about it, she made herself make sense of the dream. She wanted to know what it was, who it was, something, anything to tell Dr. Miller so they could get to the bottom of it. She'd had enough of this. Though the dream was the most terrifying part of her existence, she was very tired of living a defeated life, depressed, moody, angry, out of sorts.

As she lay there concentrating on the nightmare, she tried out several scenarios in her mind. She couldn't say the blackness that had engulfed her was anything tangible, but why then had it scared her so? Was it a wall? A cloud? Water? A person? A man? A rapist? Her husband? Her father? Her father? Her father? Her father? Was it possible? Why would she dream that? Why would she think that?

Did this person who pressed down on her have a face? Could she detect his size, weight, feel, smell? She could not, but now she had pushed herself past an imaginary line. Every time she thought of the dream, she pictured a man pressing down on her. She fought the idea that it could have been her father, but soon she could think of nothing else.

When she reported this at her next counseling session, she sensed she had finally become the perfect patient. Now they were getting somewhere. "I want you," Dr. Miller said, "to close your eyes and tell me the dream again."

She winced. "Do I have to?"

"I should think you'd want to. This may very well be the key to your recovery, Jennie. Let's pursue it. You're safe here."

"I know."

She closed her eyes and slowly began to recount the dream. "Nothing leads up to it," she said. "I think the sky goes from blue to like white or yellow, and I'm lying on my back."

"So perhaps the sky becomes the ceiling with a light on?"

"Uh-huh, and then the sky, well I guess the ceiling, the room, gets dark."

"Someone has turned off the light?"

"I guess. Anyway, it's dark and I'm still lying there."

"Are you comfortable?"

"Uh-huh. It's like I'm not even aware of anything bad."

"How old are you?"

"Oh, it's now. I see myself as if it's now, with me a grown-up adult and everything."

"Really?"

"Yeah, is that wrong?"

"It's *your* dream. Go ahead."

"Maybe it's so frightening because I'm actually a little girl?"

"Stay with the way you dreamt it this week."

"Well, suddenly what little light is left in the sky—"

"The room?"

"Yeah, the ceiling, is blocked out."

"Until then you could still see, even though it got dark?"

"Yeah, that's why I didn't imagine someone turning off a light, because it would have been totally dark then while my eyes got used to it. Anyway, something blocks my vision and I sense something huge is hovering above me."

"Some *thing* or some *one*?"

"Some thing. It is big and heavy and pressing down on me and I can't move or breathe."

"But it's not a person?"

Jennie still had her eyes closed. "No, I can't honestly say that it is." She was beginning to feel more and more uncomfortable, something playing at the edge of her mind. Something threatening. The fear was close.

"But didn't you say that when you couldn't sleep and thought about it, you were able to personify it somewhat?"

"Yes," she said quickly, beginning to panic. "But you just want the dream the way I dreamed it, right?"

"Yes, okay."

Jennie was abruptly overcome. She opened her eyes wide with terror. The feeling of oppression, of something pressing down on her had washed over her. "Oh, no!" she said, "oh, please, not while I'm awake."

She shuddered and hid her face with her hands as Dr. Miller hurried to her. She grabbed him, pulling him close for protection. "Margaret," he called to his secretary, "could you come in here, please?"

Jennie was embarrassed. She gradually released her grip. "It's okay. I'm okay. I just felt it again. It was as if I was having the dream all over again and I wasn't even asleep."

"Can I get you something?" the secretary asked, handing her a tissue.

"No. I'm okay now."

But she wasn't and she knew Dr. Miller could tell. "Tell me more about what you just went through," he said, returning to his chair as Margaret left the room.

She shook her head. "I'm trying. I just don't know." And she broke into sobs.

"Take a moment," he said. "We're in no hurry." He let her sit there and weep and she felt herself sliding into a deeper depression. Shouldn't this be a hopeful sign? Weren't they near something key here? All she could think of what a mess her idyllic little existence had become.

When she had finally composed herself, he gently probed again. "Jennie, your conscious mind is not allowing you to deal with something very important. In my opinion your mental defenses are so strong that we're not going to be able to connect this nightmare to the root causes of your problem without hypnosis."

She became convinced
that her subconscious would
reveal something she
had been repressing.

"I don't believe in that mumbo jumbo and I don't think it would work anyway," she said quickly.

"Oh, Jennie, I've seen hypnosis do marvelous things in people's lives. Your subconscious keeps perfect time; it records your memories without bias and without inhibition. The missing link in your recovery could be just below the surface. When you're willing, let me know."

It was two weeks before Jennie became willing. She did a lot of reading about hypnosis therapy—all success stories, because the literature was provided by Dr. Miller—and she became convinced that her subconscious would reveal something she had been repressing. She knew Phil would feel even more strongly than she had that this approach was bunk, so she did not tell him. Meanwhile, their fights grew more frequent and nasty. By the time she showed up for the hypnosis, she had convinced herself it would save her marriage.

Jennie proved to be an easy subject. She quickly slipped into a hypnotic state, and Dr. Miller gently walked her back mentally through her life. She was always fully conscious and aware of what was going on, and she was warmed and thrilled by the feelings of youth and freedom that came as they retrogressed through her marriage. She was a young mother, then she was a childless wife, then a newlywed, happy, carefree, in love.

She couldn't keep from smiling and remembering. And she was indeed remembering things she hadn't thought about for ages. Time alone with Phil, plans, dreams, his attentiveness, their jokes and pet names for each other, things that had been lost in the busyness of family life.

Now they were engaged, then courting, then dating, then just friends. Now they had just met and had crushes on each other. She remembered a bit of a scene with her parents over this new boyfriend. She was too young, they said, to get serious. But she felt she was falling in love and that they would come around. Apparently they had.

Now she was in high school, popular, attractive, smart, involved. She had gone to a public high school and so took some abuse for being too straight, not smoking or drinking or sleeping around. She was known as a church girl, not a party girl. Dr. Miller probed her feelings on that. She realized she was admitting for the first time that she was embarrassed and sometimes wished she did know what the real world was all about. But in the end she was pleased that she had been spared that experience.

Soon she was a junior higher with a changing body, braces. Then she remembered her first period and how grateful she was that her mother had prepared her for it and had also told her the facts of life. At first this news repulsed her.

"Why does it bother you?" Dr. Miller asked.

"Because it's so gross," she said, feeling like a sixth-grader again. "I wouldn't want anybody to do that to me."

"Do what to you?"

"You know. Sex."

"But isn't sex something you do *with* someone? Why do you say it's something that is done *to* you?"

"Well, yeah, I know, but when you 'do' it, the male does it to you."

"How do you know?"

"My mom told me."

"That the man does it to you?"

"Well, she just explained it, that's all. She said it was good and right and beautiful and God's idea and all that, but I still wouldn't want to do it. It's gross."

"Because?"

"Because I'm twelve!"

"Has anyone tried to do anything like that to you?"

"No way!"

They regressed through elementary school, Jennie recalling for the first time in a long time her new teachers, first days of class, embarrassing moments in gym class, social *faux pas,* breaking her arm in fourth grade, receiving Christ at summer Bible camp, learning to write in cursive, being sick in class during first grade, taking the bus to school for the first time.

"My mom is walking me to the bus," she said. "I want to cry so bad."

"Because?"

"Because I spend every day with her and now I have to be away from her every morning. But she keeps telling me that she will be waiting for me at the same place when I get off the bus and that I have to be brave and do well and that Jesus will be with me."

"How do you feel about that?"

"I can't believe I'm not crying. I can't smile, but I will not cry."

"You may cry now if you wish."

And she did, great torrents of tears. "Oh, I miss my mommy," she said. "Several of the other kids are crying in class, most of them boys, but I would not and I did not."

"But that is hard?"

"Very hard."

"How long did that last?"

She brightened. "The next day I couldn't wait to get on the bus, and by the end of the week I was telling my mom she didn't have to see me off at the corner. That's when *she* cried."

Dr. Miller chuckled softly. "Let's go back another year," he said. "You're four. What is your life like?"

"Saying goodbye to Daddy every morning. Playing. Lots of time with Mom. We have fun."

"Anything else?"

Jennie stopped. She shook her head.

"What?"

"Nothing. I just, I mean, that's it. That's my life."

"You had so much detail before this. Is there something you want to tell me?"

"No."

"Are you sure?"

"I think so."

"You're still four. Anything?"

"My parents are gone on a trip to Florida. They will be gone a week and come back with souvenirs, a glass with the name of a hotel on it and a real coconut."

"Who's staying with you?"

"My grandparents."

"How is that?"

"It's all right. They're great, but once my grandmother made me make up with my sister after a fight by having me kiss her on the cheek. Yuck."

"Why is that yuck?"

"They just don't know that we don't do that. Girls kissing girls! Yuck."

"Do your parents kiss you?"

"Sure! All the time! But not girls."

"All the time?"

"Well, I mean kissing goodbye and good night and stuff like that."

"What other stuff like that?"

"Nothing. Just regular stuff moms and dads kiss kids for. I really miss my mom."

"Not your dad?"

"Oh, sure, but mostly my mom because Daddy is gone every day anyway."

"Is there any other reason you don't miss your dad?"

"Not that I can think of."

"But there might be?"

"I don't know. I don't think so."

"All right, now you're three. Tell me about your life."

"Wait. I'm still four and my mom is in the hospital. She was gonna have a baby only she didn't and everybody's sad about it."

_____

"Who's taking care of you and your sister?"

"My dad."

"And how is that?"

"It's okay, but he has to have Grandma and Grandpa come when he visits Mom. I just want her home."

"Anything else?"

"Nope."

"Ready for age three?"

Jennie was silent.

"What did they call you when you were four?"

"Lots of stuff. Jennifer, Jenn, Jennie. Daddy called me Jenny June Bug." She laughed.

"Jennifer, you're three."

She was silent. Then, "I just don't remember."

"Sure you do. There's something you want to tell me."

She shook her head. "Nope. Don't remember."

"Tell me about the room going dark."

Jennie was aware she was in Dr. Miller's office, that she was under hypnosis, that she had dredged up a lot of memories, mostly innocent and easy ones, and that in reality she was an adult. But she was in this never-never land of childhood, racking her brain to remember something, anything around age three or four, but she had hit a brick wall. Was it simply because most people don't remember much before age four, or was she repressing something, even in hypnosis?

"I don't remember."

"Someone has come into the room where you're lying on your back. Who is it?"

"I don't know. I can't see him."

"Him?"

"Her, whatever. I can't see. The room is darker."

"Is it daytime or nighttime?"

"It's nap time."

"Did the room get darker because someone came in and shut the door?"

"Yeah."

"Who is it?"

"I don't know. Daddy?"

"Is it?"

She shrugged.

"What is he doing?"

"I don't know, but I can't breathe! I can't move! Something's pressing me down! Help me!"

Jennie wanted out of this state. She was reliving the nightmare. She wanted help, but she felt stuck as a child, powerless and struggling.

"Some *thing* is pressing down on you? Or some *one?*"

"Someone! Daddy!" And now she screams and cries and thrashes. Dr. Miller awakens her and lets her cry on his shoulder as his secretary looks on.

Jennie is already doubting her own mind. "It couldn't have been my father," she said. "It had to be someone else."

"The subconscious mind is a marvelous tool," Dr. Miller said. "Frankly, I think we have found the missing link, the key to your recovery. If you remember it, it is true. It happened. That's the way the mind works."

Jennie is exhausted and frazzled. What she wants more than anything is for her husband to come and pick her up, but he would have to bring the girls and it's a school night. Somehow she drives home on her own, but when she gets there she's a wreck. Phil puts the girls to bed and insists on a briefing from his agitated wife. It is the most attentive she has seen him in months, and she's convinced that she must appear to him on the edge of a breakdown. Which is precisely how she feels.

She reveals everything to him, and as the "truth" spills out about the nightmares, he doesn't even act offended that she kept them from him. He embraces her and lets her talk. Now she's certain that he is also scared for her and worried about her. By the time she gets to the part about her father raping her at age four when her mother was in the hospital with a miscarriage, she has built up anger and resentment and blame and has laid at his feet the blame for everything that has gone wrong in her life and marriage.

Phil stiffens. "Jennie!" he says. "You're telling me that my father-in-law, Stanton Beckett, molested his own daughter? Give me a break!"

"It's true," she said. "It all came back to me tonight."

"I don't believe it!"

"I didn't either, but it's true. Talk to Dr. Miller. He'll tell you!"

"I will!"

Phil called Dr. Miller right then, and by the time he got off the phone he had been educated. Many similar cases mirror this one, from the repression to the idealization to the truth coming out in hypnosis. Before long, Phil is as angry and militant as Jennie is. He begins going to counseling with her and they attempt to rebuild their marriage and life in spite of this horror.

Subsequent sessions with Dr. Miller further detail the acts of the father and tighten Jennie and Phil's understanding and resolve. They read all they can about incest and its survivors. They tell their friends and their pastor, and they note that they are closer than ever because of this trauma.

Jennie finds herself more assertive, able to express anger and speak her mind. With their therapist they plan a confrontation with her parents. Her parents are invited to help "assess the family support system," but while there the father is accused by his daughter as she sits between Phil and Dr. Miller.

"This is nonsense," Mr. Beckett says. "It's not true. Sir, you or someone has brainwashed my daughter."

Dr. Miller says something quietly about a classic denial pattern. Jennie's father says to her mother, "Surely you believe me!"

She says, "I don't know what to believe. Why would she make up a story like that? And this man is a respected professional."

"So am I," the father bristles. "At least I was until just now."

The Pseudo-memory Pandemic

The bizarre but all too common true story above spiraled into chaos, as most such cases do. Jennie's sister became involved, flatly refusing to believe the charges. She was estranged from Jennie, as were the parents, of course. Jennie refused to see any of them as long as they denied what had happened.

She became active in an aggressive organization of incest survivors, and as she became more well-versed in the literature began to recall more and more incidents of abuse. A year after the confrontation she had recalled under hypnosis that both her father *and* her mother had abused her *and* her sister, sometimes with the four of them engaged in unspeakable acts together. Eventually she became convinced that not only her father but also her Sunday school teacher and her pastor were involved in secret Satan worship with ritual killings.

Jennie actually believed that at one point she had become pregnant by her father and that she had been taken out of school for several months so she could have the baby. She had repressed for years the memory of seeing that child sacrificed to Satan in the basement of her own church, while she was threatened with death if she ever revealed the truth. That, she decided, was when she retreated into one of her several alternate personalities who protected her from such harsh reality.

The turning point in Jennie's sad story came when her husband could finally no longer believe the twists and turns. He worked with her parents in documenting her life through photographs and report cards, casting serious doubt as to whether what she alleged was even possible. Among many other contradictions, the church where the satanic sacrifice was supposed to have occurred had no basement. They finally succeeded in getting Jennie to talk to a trusted and objective friend. Now, years later, she has been slowly brought to the point where she realizes that hers was a false memory. She lives in deep regret at what she dragged her family through.

As outlandish as that story may sound to you, we have heard dozens that include Satan worship and child sacrifice. There is now a nationwide pandemic of supposed sexual and satanic ritual abuse. Allegations multiply daily from people at all levels of society. Many of these allegations arise, like Jennie's, from "long-repressed" memories "discovered" during psychotherapy and hypnosis.

One of the most important practices of insight-oriented or depth-psychotherapy is the process of

"Remembering, Repeating, and Working Through."[2] Though terms and techniques may have changed over time, still today "the therapeutic work in analysis consists in the retrieval of memories"[3]..."to fill in gaps in memory...to overcome resistance due to repression."[4]

This therapeutic process, as Dr. Miller explained to Jennie, depends upon the equally foundational concept of the unconscious as "discovered" by Freud and elaborated upon by his successors. Today an unquestioned doctrine in the psychotherapy industry is the belief in a repository of memories, thoughts, and feelings recorded since birth that determine our daily life (outside our awareness). We discuss this theory of psychic determinism further in chapter 11. Such was the basis for Dr. Miller's belief that long-repressed memories can give rise to vague symptoms of anguish—thus Dr. Miller's search for such memories and all the attendant events that followed their "discovery."

We live in an age of victims with a materialistic world view that encourages us to attribute our suffering to causes outside our control. We blame anything or anyone that impacts negatively upon us, be it the economy, the government, authorities, or parents. We seek some evidence of actual harm which can then be seen as responsible for our "dysfunction." The collapsing morality of our culture, with its sordid news and the numbing violence in our entertainment, serves to validate this search for actual harm.

If we can believe pop psychologists and the headlines, then we are a nation of victims, all families are dysfunctional, and vast numbers of children are abused. Psychologists strive to connect current discomfort and past abuse, though no memory of such exists by the supposed victim or anyone else in his family. As in Jennie's case, these connections would seem ludicrous were it not for the unquestioned body of psychotherapeutic theory that seems to validate them.

Metaphors without precise or widely accepted understanding—such as "defense mechanisms" and "repression"—are tossed about to explain how any problem can result from forgotten incest.[5]

To the therapist, recovery requires that the emotion and imagery attached to the trauma be integrated into the victim's self-structure.[6] The recovery and integration of the memories is central to the resolution of the psychological trauma.[7] The job of the therapist is to help the client bring previously unremembered aspects of the trauma to the surface and to deal with their impact.[8] Hypnotic techniques are used to access memories that otherwise seem completely out of reach.[9]

Can we trust the unconscious? Are things we remember always accurate and valid? Do they reflect actual experience? The psychotherapy industry uniformly answers "yes." The average therapist is unaware that anyone is even questioning such and generally views those who express doubt as being "in denial."

Doubt is beginning to rise from within the psychology field itself. A subdiscipline of psychology—the only field in psychology accurately defined as science—attempts to apply accepted rules and methods of science to the study of the human brain. This small but growing number of researchers is concerned with the validity of the information in one's memory. They are providing a growing body of contrasting information which indicates that we have very little objective knowledge of just how the memory functions, why we forget, how we remember, or how any memories influence our lives. Interesting work is also being done on the supposed recovery of previously unknown information brought to mind during the course of insight-oriented or depth-psychotherapy, especially that using hypnosis.

The unreliability of information discovered under hypnosis became a matter of scientific inquiry and dispute early in the 1980s.[10,11] Similarly, the use in court of information retrieved in this way was seriously questioned.[12,13] It was clearly demonstrated that pseudo-memories, memories of events which never occurred, could be induced in the subject by the hypnotist.[14]

A study published in *SCIENCE* magazine in 1983 demonstrated this.[15] That author urged that "utmost caution be used whenever hypnosis is used as an investigative tool." Soon after, work began to be published which showed that current mood states could decidedly skew recollections of past events.[16] This type of research has also proven the general unreliability of autobiographical information.[17] Other studies have repeatedly shown that people in depth counseling or under hypnosis really do believe and hold onto memories that have been given or subtly encouraged.[18]

The impact of this on courtroom testimony interested Elizabeth Loftus, Ph.D., who describes herself as having "spent 20 years of my professional career trying to dispel the myth that human memory is infallible and immune from distortion."[19]

Numerous studies have shown the ease with which

suggestible people can be induced to have pseudo-memories even without hypnosis.[20] These also show that such memories are truly persistent.[21] If the therapist develops good rapport with the client such that there is desire to please and behave appropriately on the part of the client, the stage is set for the creation of pseudo-memories.[22] The person most susceptible to pseudo-memories is the one who is anxious, suggestible, and involved in a therapy context where such outcomes are expected. If the created memories are found to reduce anxiety, they seem to be reinforced and are even more likely to be perceived long term as true memories.[23]

Keep the above in mind as you think back on Jennie's experience. Perhaps, as a lay person, you were subtly swept along as her memories of childhood trauma slowly emerged. But consider what was really happening in that counseling situation:

First, her initial hunch that her problems stemmed from common, modern complaints was on target. She needed a frank discussion with her husband, and they both likely needed true spiritual refreshment. It was probable that their daily devotional lives had waned, and they had begun taking God and each other for granted. Her low-grade depression symptoms indicated that she was feeling guilty about something, probably her own inconsistency spiritually. We don't want to downplay her very real feelings of angst, but the jump from harried homemaker to abused child was a huge one subtly engineered—albeit earnestly—by a counselor.

We would go so far as to argue that counseling either spouse alone is a prescription for marital disaster.

We also believe it was a mistake for the counselor to look for the "reasons" Jennie was doing what she was doing. Rather, he should have concentrated on the actions themselves and looked at them in the light of Scripture so she could confess them as sin and repent.

Jennie was on target when she first suspected that her husband should share some responsibility for their squabbles. Clearly, these were relationship problems common to most marriages and can most likely be solved if both parties work together. Jennie alone was taking the blame, and the counselor was allowing it.

We believe it was a mistake for the counselor, a trusted authority, to tell a suggestible client that "it may get darker before dawn." A statement from such an authority figure makes it sure to happen, whether necessary or not.

Jennie was further subjugated by Dr. Miller when he assured her husband in her presence that he would "not allow" any husband-bashing. That put her in a demeaning, vulnerable, little-girl position.

Dr. Miller did the right thing in leaving his office door open and having his secretary close by. That indicates that he is appropriate in his dealings with clients. Such a procedure, however, did not keep him from making serious errors in judgment.

He implanted in her the idea that there were areas that needed to be explored that she might not want to share with her husband. Of course, he was only asking. We are not accusing him of malice in this, but certainly recklessness.

Throughout her therapy, he guided her into new areas. Eventually one of his prescriptions was to, in essence, honor herself. Any form of self-love and self-worship is not of God and can lead only to destruction.

The conclusion that Jennie's discomfort was due to a problem with authority figures was a long stretch as well. Many women have similar problems with husband or boss, and the general category of so-called male authority has little to do with it. Such interpretations can serve to ensure that Jennie would not act out some insubordination to the authority of the counselor.

◆

> *False memories are created in clients who seek self-understanding, personal growth, or simply relief from some discomfort.*

Every conclusion Jennie came to, up to and especially including the "meaning" of her nightmare, was planted. As she grew more and more dependent upon and trusting of the counselor, she talked herself into all manner of new truths. Her nightmare itself may have simply been the result of mounting pressure in her marriage. Ironically, it may have even represented the pressure she felt from the counselor.

Most of all, she had been encouraged to see the minor human frailties of her father—certainly fewer and less serious than most—as cause for a most heinous suspicion.

Even in the face of scientific evidence casting grave doubt on the validity and ethics of searching for "discovered" memories, the devotees of psychotherapy persist in these old views of the mind concocted by Freud 100 years ago and which form the foundation for this travesty of health care.

This modern-day debacle was actually experienced even by Freud himself early in his career. In an 1897 letter to Wilhelm Fliess, his friend and intellectual confidant-collaborator, he himself cast great doubt on the reliability of memories retrieved from the unconscious. At the same time, he revealed some of the damage done by practicing such retrieval.[24]

Over the following years, however, Freud vacillated and sometimes still attached importance to the supposed facts described by the "remembering" client.[25] Clearly, we should seriously question the credibility of individuals who have discovered in psychotherapy that they were abused in their forgotten past. This is especially true when there is no corroborating evidence or witness. False memories are created in clients like Jennie who seek self-understanding, personal growth, or simply relief from some discomfort. The client is anxious, trusting, suggestible and, of course, seeks to be a "good patient."

The therapist does not usually seek corroboration for new memories, as this is not required by the theory upon which the therapy is based. Emphasis on evidence is, in fact, viewed as destructive to the therapeutic relationship. Unconditional acceptance of what the patient says is claimed to be of great importance. The therapist sees no reason to doubt the patient's autobiographical information, and from his training is convinced that parents are to blame for most of our suffering emotionally as adults. Like Freud himself, the therapist is unsure whether the difference between fact and symbol is an important distinction anyway. In psychotherapeutic circles it is not uncommon to hear, "A client's perception *is* his reality." Thus the absurd conclusion: If the patient believes he was abused, that is what is important, whether the abuse was real or not!

As in Jennie's case, rarely does confrontation with the alleged abuser achieve any resolution. Actual abusers deny the charges, while the falsely accused are stunned, overwhelmed and, of course, also deny the charges. The therapist usually then mandates a break between the patient (now defined as an adult victim of child abuse) and the abuser, who is most often an otherwise respectable father of the client. The parent is said to be "in denial," and the therapist easily convinces the angry patient that only a complete cessation of normal family relationships will ever cause the parent to confess.

Now bereft of family, the original victim is left to continue therapy and to participate in victim-support groups for social and emotional support. In such groups, the victims tell and retell their stories of abuse, supposedly for the purpose of "helping one another." The false memories take on increased clarity and the imagery becomes more vivid every time the story is repeated. Either during private therapy sessions or during the process of relaying the story to support groups, lurid tales of so-called satanic ritual abuse are often revealed. Thus the victim follows a path decidedly away from any resolution with family.

This scenario is thoroughly consistent with and to be expected from insight-oriented psychotherapy as it has been practiced since first invented a century ago. In fact, failure to search for and address these "fragments of memory" or telltale signs of repressed early abuse is viewed as "compromising treatment."[26] In a fashion similar to the diagnosis of so-called Multiple Personality Disorder, therapists are trained and expected to seek out the "hidden connections" of early life abuse as explanation for the uncomfortable lives of their patients. Because of the basis for the practice of psychotherapy, the nature of the therapeutic relationship, and the needs of the patient, it should not be surprising that something is concocted out of nothing.[27]

We live in a violent world, and there are many cases of actual abuse of children at the hands of the parents. For the most part, these are cases with physical evidence and eyewitness accounts. The abusers are often recognizable in their many behavioral and emotional difficulties. Nothing in these pages should be interpreted as doubting the realities of our fallen nature or as lacking compassion for those hurt by it. Our concern is over the particularly vile abuse of patients and families as perpetrated by the psychotherapy industry.

Like Jennie, a growing number of adult children have come to realize they were drawn into a lie and have thus recanted the accusations made on the basis of previously repressed memories.

The families falsely accused are amazingly similar:

They are usually middle or upper class where the children are able to pay a therapist.

The alleged abuser is almost exclusively the father, but increasingly, as the tale becomes more lurid, the mother or even siblings move from "enablers" to "co-abusers."

The victims are usually daughters ranging in age from 25 to 45 who discovered their memories while in therapy for some vague discomfort.

The parents accused are almost always free of any suggestion that would give rise to real suspicion that they could be abusers.

There is never a witness nor is there a history of physical evidence.

More often than not, the retrieved story, if true, would have required a degree of privacy not feasible in the family home.

Regularly, siblings offer no corroboration unless also subjected to psychotherapeutic assistance to discover their own memories. As a result, the siblings are included in the therapeutic shunning pursued by the supposed victim on the advice of the therapist.

Sadly, most of these families have little or no contact with their daughters for years, if ever again. Most of the families suffer in secret. Some confront the therapist only to be labeled as "in denial." Recently, many of these families are courageously banding together to warn others of what appears to be the latest abuse by the psychotherapeutic industry. They are slowly beginning to understand that this type of result is inherent in the very nature of psychotherapy.

Bible passages related to the false memory controversy:

- The requirement of witnesses—Deuteronomy 19:15, 1 Timothy 5:19

- The discipline process related to an offense—Matthew 18:15-17

- Admonition regarding focusing on the past—Philippians 3:13-15, Luke 9:62, Isaiah 26:3, 43:18, 65:16

- Revenge/Justice—Revelation 6:10-11, Malachi 3:14-18, Luke 18:1-8, Romans 12:17

- Self-pity—Philippians 2:1-18, Isaiah 53:3, Psalm 22, Matthew 11:28

- Are we victims or sinners?—Isaiah 64:6, Psalm 103, Romans 3:9-20, Psalm 14:1-3, 1 Samuel 2:25, Romans 5:12-21, Psalm 51, Galatians 5:19-21

4

Grace's Persecution

◆————————◆

NEARLY EVERY DETAIL of our first case study came from the real-life Jennie herself, because she eventually returned to reality after getting proper counsel. The story of Grace (also a pseudonym), however, has been pieced together from her own written record and from others who encountered her. You will see in the end why she would not have cooperated with recreating this account for the purposes we are about in this book. We have—of course—again camouflaged as much as possible to make her identity impossible to detect.

Grace, 28 and single, was an assistant professor of English literature at a small liberal arts college in the Midwest. She described herself as an avid reader, able to lose and transport herself in the images and feelings of the stories she read. Her passion for literature, particularly that of the rural South, came through in her classes, where for the last two years she had been voted teacher of the year.

The chairman of her department, however, was a late-middle-aged Englishman, an Oxford graduate she found intelligent and wise in his field, but aloof, stuffy, and none too complimentary. When Grace occasionally fished hard enough for his assessment of her work or even some acknowledgment of her popularity, she was not pleased with his response.

"Frankly," he had been known to say, "as entertaining as the great Southern Gothic writers may have been, they are not truly English writers, as it were. The influence of Christianity is more culturalized with them, their earthy—shall we say guttural—flights of graphic fantasy don't hold a candle to the true classics from across the pond. As for Grace's teacher of the year awards, let's remember that these reflect the thoughts of late-adolescent romantics who love to be catered to and entertained. I would rank her about in the middle of the department, or even lower due to her favored choice of reading material—which I find banal."

Grace's employment record, she was fond of lamenting to co-workers, was full of references to her seeming lack of inclination toward research or scholarly writing. She had been proud of being published in small literary magazines on the storytelling traditions behind Southern American literature. To a few friends she even let it be known that she hoped her teaching awards and the publishing credit would qualify her for a recently announced associate professorship opening that included tenure. "Wouldn't that be a neat way to celebrate my sixth year here?" she said.

Grace let it be known among her confidants that she sincerely did not see any of her colleagues as ready for the appointment, and as the day neared for the announcement of the department head's choice, she grew more and more excited. Normally plain in appearance, she began dressing a bit more nattily and was even seen with a salon hairdo and a touch of makeup.

One of her friends asked her on the big day how her interviews and the screening process had gone. "I was never interviewed," she said.

"Then don't get your hopes up. You don't really expect a promotion and raise and tenure without some interaction, do you?"

"I've sent him my updated resumé," she said, thumbing in the direction of the department head's closed office door.

Just then the door swung open and all eyes were on the department chairman and the widely considered rather dull Daniel, a colleague of Grace's. He emerged pumping the old man's hand and assuring him, "I won't let you down, sir. And thank you! I've got to call my wife."

Grace was seen raising her eyebrows to Daniel as he swept past, as if to ask what was up. He merely pumped a fist in the air and whispered, "Yes! Yes!"

That afternoon the entire department was called together for the anticlimactic announcement of the news that had already swept the campus. "Daniel's responses to my queries were what we were hoping to hear. As you all know, his analysis of the influence of Puritanism on English literature won our campus, and may I say our department, national recognition. We've found him a worthy candidate and the board has voted to approve my recommendation for his promotion."

Grace was able to produce polite, frozen-smile applause as the younger members of the department hooted and clapped Daniel on the back and enjoyed congratulatory cake. Grace went home in a funk. She told friends that Daniel was only average in every way she could think of. "I cannot understand why he was promoted over me. I mean, that thing he wrote for the Liberal Arts Review was okay, but he's never been voted best prof, let alone two years in a row."

Though clearly angry and hurt, Grace did not bad-mouth the decision outside her small circle of acquaintances. They noticed, however, that she was growing increasingly bitter and seemed to take a different approach to her work. For the next month her personal habits and discipline seemed to wane. She cared less and less about how far in advance she prepared her lectures, often canceling class or giving easy assignments. She dressed more sloppily as the days wore on, and more than one colleague noticed she was not eating well. Always thin and pale, she began looking gaunt. Her baggy clothes hung on her.

She muttered to one friend that she wished she had the courage to tell the department head what she really felt about how he and all the other men at the school had treated her. "But I won't," she said. "He'll criticize me and I'll sit there and take it like a good little girl. Face it, it's a man's world."

The next day, as she sat waiting for her monthly appointment with the department head, she noticed the secretary staring at her. "Excuse me," she said, when Grace looked up, "but may I ask you something? Is something bothering you? You look a little, I don't know, down lately."

Later Grace would admit that she didn't know what got into her, but for some reason she uncharacteristically opened up to a woman she had never before conversed with beyond pleasantries. "Frankly, I have been feeling badly lately and mixed up about a lot of things."

"Do you think it could be depression?" the secretary asked.

"I wouldn't know if it's clinical or not," Grace said, "but I'm depressed all right. Isn't every woman depressed who's attending or working at Men First College?"

The secretary smiled. "I think he'll be ready for you in a couple of minutes, but let me just recommend someone to you." She wrote out the name and phone number of a counselor, a woman she said she trusted and who had "been wonderful for me."

"Wonderful how?"

"I don't have time to get into all the details, but let me tell you, she healed me of my past, helped me grow into a healthier self, and transformed my life."

"My goodness," Grace said. "All that?"

"Believe it or not."

Something in Grace must have believed it, because after another depressing and humiliating monthly encounter with her boss, she was ready for some healing. From the first session, Grace was drawn to this warm, caring, motherly counselor, Marlene Lansing. Marlene listened, she was interested, and she seemed to understand the pain and frustration in Grace's life. When Grace occasionally blamed her troubles on "this man's world," Marlene merely smiled and nodded sympathetically.

"I'm interested in all that," she told her, "but tell me who you are, where you're from, how you grew up."

"My story is boring," Grace told her.

"Try me. It'll help me get to know you and help you."

Grace took a deep breath and rattled off the details. "Fourth of four daughters, blue collar family, Dad worked all the time, his whole life at the same plant. I'm the only daughter who graduated college, and I had to pay my own way. Happy enough childhood. Had friends, cousins, went on vacations, to movies, read a lot. Loved to tell stories, would make up whoppers to entertain the family."

"Boyfriends?"

"I didn't date."

"Really? Why?"

"I don't know. I wasn't asked."

"Did you make yourself available?"

"I didn't know how. I was kinda plain, didn't get contact lenses till college, probably seemed like a bookworm. I didn't go for all the social junk. Didn't like sports and school parties and all that. I keep thinking some day Prince Charming will come and sweep me off my feet."

"You're very attractive."

"Well, thanks, but I don't feel it and apparently men don't see me that way."

"Church?"

"My parents are lifers. We went every Sunday. I never liked it, never got into it. We don't talk about it. I mean, they went, but they never made a big devout deal of it. They don't even ask me if I still go, which I don't. I don't think I've gone to church since I was in high school."

"You miss it?"

"Nope."

"Tell me about your father."

"He's been dead a couple of years. I hardly knew him. I talked to him more the last three Christmases before he died than I ever did as a child. I was his last hope for a son, you know, and they say when he found out I was a girl he said, 'My luck.'"

"Ouch. You say, 'when he found out.' Was he not in the delivery room? Weren't they doing that by the sixties?"

"They might have been, but not Mr. Macho. I guess he waited and paced, and that night he still worked his shift. He was always working."

"So no real relationship with your father?"

Grace laughed. "That's an understatement."

"How about your mother?"

"We're still close."

"Still? You mean you've always been?"

"Oh, yeah. She says I kept her young, as the baby, you know. She's not an educated woman and she was impressed as she could be when I started getting good grades and writing and telling stories. She was always the one who egged me on to entertain at family gatherings. I was always her 'smart one,' her 'college bound' one. 'Gonna be an author or a doctor or a professor or somethin',' she'd always say."

"She sounds wonderful."

"The best."

"That's quite a disparity between your views of your mother and your father."

Grace shrugged. "Win a few, lose a few," she said.

"What does that mean?"

"You know. You take the bad with the good. Lord knows I've had my share of bad for whatever can be said about the good things in my life."

"Oh, a lot of good things may be said about your life," Marlene said. She ran down a litany of educational and career accomplishment, to which Grace sat shaking her head. "Why is this uncomfortable for you?" Marlene asked.

"My life is a mess! I don't care about my classes, my appearance, my health. I can't stand my boss or my colleagues. I feel like I'm low woman on the totem pole in a male-dominated world. If there was so much for me to be proud or happy about, I wouldn't be here."

"I'm assuming you're here because you want to get better."

"I am."

"And you will. Tell me what is bothering you the most."

Once Grace began she couldn't stop. It was as if she had spent a lifetime keeping score. She recounted insults, slights, and offenses throughout her life. Almost all of these were perpetrated by males, from boy cousins and elementary school classmates to teens and adults—primarily, of course, her father.

"How did you fight back and defend yourself?"

"I didn't."

"Why not?"

"I felt powerless. No one would believe me. I just kept it all inside."

"It's coming out now."

"I know. And I don't like it. I don't like myself this way."

"That's a start."

Over the next several weeks Grace continued with her complaints that she felt like a doormat, always volunteering to help but never getting thanks or recognition.

"But you were voted—"

"Teacher of the year, yeah, twice. But remember my classes are mostly women students, and, like my department head says, those kinds of awards don't amount to much."

"They meant a lot to you."

———————◆———————

> *"I think if you search yourself*
> *and consider what you had*
> *and did not have as a child,*
> *you can see how your past*
> *affects your present."*

"But not to anyone else. In fact, it would have almost been better not to have received them than to get them and have them denigrated by a man in authority over me."

"Have you ever been able to ask for recognition by reminding your boss of your value to the department?"

"Never. That would be demeaning. Anyway, men are so inconsiderate!"

"That's a given we all suffer under," Marlene said. "I want to pursue a few other basic areas with you." Marlene probed areas of Grace's past that related to unmet developmental needs: love, affection, hugging, security, quality time, bonding. The answers, of course, established an unsurprising pattern. She received all this from her mother. Her late father remained a shadowy, peripheral character.

After several sessions of such depressing revelations, Grace asked for an assessment. "This is not my field," she admitted. "What does all this say about me?"

"Well," Marlene began carefully, "I generally like to have you come to these realizations and discoveries yourself. I think if you search yourself and consider what you had and did not have as a child, you can see how your past affects your present."

"Good mom, bad dad, you mean?"

"That's not how I would phrase it, but that's the bottom line. The question is, how bad?"

"What do you mean?"

"Well, to be frank, you are manifesting typical behavior patterns of individuals whose inner children were emotionally starved by one or both parents."

"But I don't feel as if I care that I was never close to my father."

"And we need to find out why. That's probably an adult defense mechanism to keep it from hurting on the surface, but obviously it's hurting inside and manifesting itself every day."

"Obviously. So where do we go from here?"

"I think you're ready to proceed. Stay with me now. Your hurting inner child needs to be attended to. If she can be re-programmed, a healthier self can emerge."

"How does that happen?"

"It's not easy, and only you can decide if it will be worth it."

"I'll try anything to keep from going on like this. I can only assume you know what you're doing, and I've seen at least one good result from your work—our department secretary."

"Here's what we'll do. We'll conduct a search for hidden memories of bad conditioning or even outright abuse. These will have to be safely restored to a healthier self so you can attain your true self, be relieved of the inner pain, and be transformed into the kind of an adult you were meant to be."

"Wait a minute. I haven't hidden any memories. All I remember about my father I told you. He was always working. He never abused me or anything like that. I don't think he ever even spanked me. He just didn't have much time for us girls, but lots of fathers are like that. I never liked him much but I didn't hate him either. I figure he was just a typical man."

Marlene continued as if Grace had said nothing. "These memories cannot be simply regained and talked about. They will have to be relived, re-experienced with all the feelings, emotions, and pain with which they were originally experienced."

"You're assuming I have hidden memories."

"Only through this revivification process can true inner healing take place."

"But what if there is nothing there?"

"Let me just say this: I have had untold numbers of clients who have been healed of unmet needs they were totally unaware of. If you remembered them, you would likely have dealt with them and they wouldn't be ruining your life now."

That certainly made sense. Grace left feeling as if she were the perfect candidate for this tried-and-proved method of recovery. And she was. As the months rolled by, Grace was deep into therapy. Through a careful process, Marlene Lansing was able to uncover and even predict memories of hurts and deprivation, mostly the fault of Grace's father, going back years and years.

Eventually these sessions became emotional and scary as Grace not only dredged up particularly painful memories, but was also able to relive them. There was much emotion, tears, trembling, crying, and sometimes even screaming out for the love and affection she was supposedly robbed of by her father. She felt strangely transformed by these encounters, as if she was free to be a needy child again. She was convinced she had reconnected with her inner child and was allowing her to speak her mind.

Marlene was always there to masterfully guide, suggest, reassure, and comfort. She was able to explain and make sense of it all. She explained that these long-forgotten memories were the cause of Grace's current problems and that they would soon be on the road to a new Grace.

One momentous session occurred when Grace was able to regress all the way back to her birth. She had the sensation of being pushed and squeezed out through a dark, warm, wet tunnel and emerging into blinding light. She screamed like a newborn and then tearfully described an out-of-body experience. She was floating near the ceiling and was suddenly out in the waiting room where her father stood when a nurse called his name.

"She's telling him it's another girl," Grace said pitifully, "and he's shaking his head and smiling, but he's not happy. He's saying, 'Wouldn't you know? Just my luck!' He's disgusted and dissatisfied! And I'm the reason!"

With that she collapsed into sobs so heart-wrenching that Marlene held her and rocked her and wept with her. Before the end of the session Grace asked, "Was that real? Could I remember my own birth?"

"It happens," Marlene said. "Just because you couldn't process it then doesn't mean you can't retrieve and re-experience it now. It was lodged there in your memory, which never lies. Lady, you have discovered the pivot point upon which your life revolves. How do you feel?"

"Unwanted, unloved, unmet."

"And?"

"And I was always trying to please my never-accepting, too-busy, never-truly-loving father."

"All your achievements were for him? Not for your mother?"

"She loved me unconditionally. She encouraged me, yes. But I was secure in her love even if I failed. It was all for him, and he never cared."

Armed with the insights from those memories, Grace and Marlene embarked on a rebuilding process. Marlene took her back again to that birth experience and even before to the point where she felt loved and secure in her mother's womb. In contrast to seeing her father's look of disgust at the news she was a girl, she now was able to relive her mother's caresses and baby talk as she nursed for the first time and was cherished.

After rebuilding and solidifying her security in at least one parent, Grace was walked through a process of letting her inner child speak her mind to her father, to scream at him, to plead with him, to tell him off.

Marlene soon encouraged Grace to devote herself to rebuilding her personality from the inside even between sessions. Marlene gave her a long list of books to read on building self-esteem, inner healing, and healing damaged emotions. Her assignment was to transform her very self from a doormat to a self-assured, assertive, self-aware, modern woman. Marlene also placed her in a recovery group composed of other women with similarly horrible histories of neglect and abuse.

One particularly important breakthrough took place when she was able, in front of the group, to unilaterally forgive her dead father for all the wrongs he had perpetrated against her and all his offenses of omission, like robbing her of the security and attention she so needed from him. He was, she had come to realize, just another victim of the same cold, male-dominated world she was raised in and in which she was now forced to work and compete.

Grace was clearly changing. She was becoming assertive and self-controlled. On campus she became involved in faculty women's groups concerned with issues of academia and their ascent within the power structure of higher education. It wasn't long before she was encouraged to initiate a discrimination complaint against her department chairman. With one of the most powerful and successful Equal Employment Opportunity counselors on campus to help her, she won the case. To make the victory all the more delicious, not only was she promoted to associate professor with retroactive pay back to when Daniel had been promoted, but she received tenure *and* all the men in the English Lit department were required to attend 40 hours of gender sensitivity training.

Her many activities concerning rights, women's issues, multi-culturalism, and the advancement of female authors in her department's curriculum began taking more and more of her time. She still enjoyed teaching, but she felt more alive and self-actualized than ever while spending time as a women's activist.

Gone were the days of self-pity and keeping feelings buried. Her sessions with Marlene Lansing more often than not were given over to recounting victories over injustice. Grace was working on a plan to ferret out what she called micro-inequities, those small slights, insults, and putdowns (on the part of the men on campus), which women won't recognize as such without having their "awareness heightened."

Despite these shared victories and plans, however, she still needed input from Marlene. In her activities with other women on campus of late, particularly with her E.E.O. counselor, she had begun experiencing strong feelings of comradeship, oneness, and a kind of mutual affection she had never before encountered.

"I haven't admitted this to anyone else yet, because it scares me," she told her therapist. "But I'm beginning to wonder if I'm not a lesbian."

"And what would be so wrong with that?"

"I don't know. I've just never seen myself that way before."

"Never fantasized about it?"

"No."

"Are you closed to it?"

"I don't know. I guess I shouldn't be."

Within a month, Grace had resigned from the college and moved to a large East Coast city with her E.E.O. counselor. They work on a magazine devoted to women's issues. To close her life chapter with Marlene Lansing, she wrote a long letter thanking her for healing her inner child and for helping her discover that healthier self she was always meant to become.

5

The Healing of Memories

◆————————◆

W<small>E DISCUSSED IN CHAPTER</small> 3 one of the more flagrant disasters from the psychotherapy industry: the creation and/or implanting of false memories of early life abuse. This subject is developed even further in chapter 12.

However, our concern with memories is even broader. There is in our culture an obsession with past experiences and the supposed importance of these in a person's current life. A constant stream of information in the psychologized media stresses the need to recover our past, share our memories with a therapist, soothe the hurts of our inner child, and receive treatment for our unmet developmental needs. We are told that these memories need to be safely restored to consciousness to produce a healthier self and that the inner pain of a not-so-gentle childhood will then go away.[1]

Articles in all kinds of periodicals focus on the importance of learning "the secrets of your past."[2] These accept without question that important, influential repressed memories exist, that the retrieval of such secrets is possible and reliable, and that with the help of a therapist this will lead to a healthier, happier life. The manner in which this will happen, however, is never clearly described. "Everyone should look into their past, for the same reason that healthy people should get checked for cancer."[3] "If something bad did happen, you can get help. For a referral to a qualified therapist in your area, call..."[4]

If that advice were not convincing enough, media of all sorts publish lists of telltale signs which "may indicate" a repressed history of trauma, abuse, or deficient nurturing. This history, of course, is said to exert a negative influence on the life of the subject, thus creating those listed signs and symptoms of deep emotional distress. A bibliography of such lists would consume many pages, with items varying from the common to the ludicrous. In the same way that fortune cookie predictions could apply almost universally, these lists usually include compulsive habits (overeating, drinking, smoking), uncontrollable anger, recurring medical problems (such as stiff neck), strong aversions to particular foods or smells, and academic problems (overachieving *or* underachieving).[5]

The intent of such lists is anything but humorous. This preoccupation with the past is seen as the key to a better life: "...[people] come to therapy because they have problem[s]. The therapist can give them a way to understand how those troubles started without requiring anything from them. They can reconstruct a memory about childhood events that never happened, and can say, 'That's why I'm having this problem.' And that get[s] them off the hook; they don't have to look at themselves; they don't have to deal with their own personal responsibility. It's the oldest game in the world. It's exactly the same thing that Adam did when God came to him in the garden saying, 'What are you doing? Why do you have that fig leaf on?' Adam pointed the finger at someone else."[6]

The assumption that remembered material is accurate and reliable and necessary to the therapeutic process is foundational to the psychotherapeutic industry. The notions concocted by Freud 100 years ago are accepted as inerrant dogma within the profession. In chapter 3 we reviewed the growing body of scientific evidence that makes the reliability and usefulness of such memories not only doubtful but fatally flawed. Psychotherapy, even without hypnosis as in Grace's case, is known to have a proclivity toward the creation of false memories. In addition, the tendency of anxious or depressed people to have distorted memory is well known and documented. Considering this, the fact that anyone would trust any "healing" that relies on the search for negative memories is further evidence of man's fallen state and deceitful heart (Jeremiah 17:9).

What healing is actually claimed? Popular articles advocating the search for memories invariably encourages the reader to seek "professional help." Always unspecified is exactly what will be done with the memories when they are discovered, and certainly we are not told what will happen to the ill-fated person named as the cause of those bad memories. Vague reference is made to a "hurting inner child" or to "unmet developmental needs."

The actual techniques used in the healing process are not specified for the casual reader. Likewise, they are nowhere specified for the psychotherapist. Not advertised by the psychotherapy industry is the fact that there is no manual, no guidebook, no standard for the "healing of memories" or for any other "talking treatment," for that matter. A field devoid of uniformity in training or practice can hardly be expected to have a "right way" to heal in any area. If questioned about technique, the therapist is likely to wax poetic in terms complex but is highly unlikely to be more specific than some version of "remembering, repeating, and working through."[7] The concept of "working through" is especially vague and poorly described. At best it is portrayed as an intellectual understanding of the "why" of behavior that somehow supports and facilitates a person's ability to self-change in the future. In 100 years, there has not been one scientifically conducted, rigorous, respected study (controlled or noncontrolled) that has demonstrated the efficacy of insight-oriented or depth-psychotherapy. Since there have been scientific, well-designed studies that have shown the opposite, we should certainly question both the theories and resultant practices of psychotherapy.

This preoccupation with traumatic memories rests *solely* upon the notion that they are somehow responsible for the dissatisfactions of one's daily life. So, the search for hidden memories is actually a process by which a person can be defined as a victim. Victims are not responsible and cannot be held responsible, and thus the person with the problem has been presented with a feel-good escape from culpability.

More than any others, we Christians should question such a theory and practice. Yet in church publications, we find the same lists of telltale signs, articles that encourage the search for hidden memories, and advice regarding the need for an "experienced therapist" to heal the memories. Glowing success stories fill their pages.

The process of remembering, repeating, and working through is no different with the Christian therapists than with those of the secular except for the addition of a few forced Bible references. Churches are full of support groups for "Adult Children of . . ." As one might expect, the same outcomes prevail whether in church-based or secular therapy. We see the same creation of false memories, the same broken families, the same overreliance on continued long-term therapy and groups, the same uncertainty of results, and the same attribution of responsibility to someone else. Such methods are not helping people face their real problems and certainly do not exhibit the compassion of Christ.

The Pulley
by George Herbert

When God at first made man,
Having a glass of blessings standing by,
   "Let us," said he, "pour on him all we can;
Let the world's riches, which disperséd lie,
   Contract into a span."

So strength first made a way;
Then beauty flowed, then wisdom, honor, pleasure;
   When almost all was out, God made a stay,

Perceiving that, alone of all his treasure,
   Rest in the bottom lay.

   "For if I should," said he,
"Bestow this jewel also on my creature,
   He would adore my gifts instead of me,
And rest in Nature, not the God of Nature,
   So both should losers be.

   "Yet let him keep the rest,
But keep them with repining restlessness.
   Let him be rich and weary, that at least,
If goodness lead him not, yet weariness
   May toss him to my breast."

George Herbert was a seventeenth-century Welsh poet who gave up prestige and wealth to become a modest country preacher. His poetic picture of the origin of man's restlessness may be less than accurate, but he speaks straight from Scripture to what man should do with his "repining restlessness."

In Matthew 11:28, Jesus says, "Come to me, all you who are weary and burdened, and I will give you rest." Yet, "rich and weary," we are far more likely to toss ourselves on the psychiatrist's couch than on the breast of Jesus.

In contrast to the world, the church feels some need to defend itself for running to therapists, though that need is fading as psychology becomes integrated into doctrine. This integration is defended largely on the basis that "all truth is God's truth," and it is blithely assumed that psychological theory is truth. Even if it were, it has done what Herbert describes: caused God's creatures to adore His gifts instead of Him. The church has come to rest in what it views as science, rather than in the God of all science.

The so-called "prosperity teachers" tell us that material wealth and physical health were purchased in the atonement and are thus here for us now. Much of the church has rightfully seen this to be false and unbiblical, if for no other reason than that such promises seem to so often hinge on donations to the "faith teacher."

◆

The psychological gospel teaches that I sin because of what others have done to me, that salvation lies in raising my self-worth, and that God is a genie waiting to meet my every need.

Still, more and more of the church is buying into this heresy. Many church leaders seem ashamed of the Scriptures. Can the truth of Job 5:7 ("Yet man is born to trouble as surely as sparks fly upward.") compare with the happiness that Christian treatment centers promise?

Throughout history, Jesus' followers have hardly led healthy, wealthy, comfortable lives. Yet church history seems almost as foreign to Christian leaders today as does Scripture itself. Our heads brim with knowledge of the latest self-help technique, and we don't question that times have changed and that the new "truths" of psychology have somehow been used of God to deliver us from discomfort and give us "mental health."

The church is fast running from the Christian life depicted in Scripture. Jesus combined with His promise of rest this statement: "Take my yoke upon you and learn of me." We answer, "Yoke? That would chafe! What's this about learning of Him who was 'despised and rejected of men, a man of sorrows and familiar with suffering' (Isaiah 53:3)? I was told Jesus would make me happy. After all, He is God. He could handle that suffering and rejection, but salvation means I don't have to. I'd rather talk about 'life more abundant' than all this business of imitating the Son of Man who had nowhere to lay His head."

The psychological gospel teaches that I sin because of what others have done to me, that salvation lies in raising my self-worth, and that God is a genie waiting to meet my every need. This leads to the unbiblical view of faith being the key to tapping the powers of that celestial genie.

In contrast, the revealed Word of God says, "Now faith is being sure of what we hope for and certain of what we do not see" (Hebrews 11:1). What is this hope and certainty? The Bible doesn't say it's happy feelings, outrageous laughter, fun marriages, or freedom from guilt when we are guilty. We are promised that same hope to which Abraham and all those listed in the Faith Hall of Fame in Hebrews 11 clung to: ". . . they did not receive the things promised; they only saw them and welcomed them from a distance. And they admitted they were aliens and strangers on earth. . . . longing for a better country—a heavenly one. Therefore, God is not ashamed to be called their God, for he has prepared a city for them" (Hebrews 11: 13-15).

Did only the writer of Hebrews see things that way? Note these passages from Paul, James, and Peter:

...We rejoice in the hope of the glory of God. Not only so, but we also rejoice in our sufferings, because we know that suffering produces perseverance; perseverance, character; and character, hope. And hope does not disappoint us (Romans 5:2,3).

Consider it pure joy, my brothers, when you face trials of many kinds, because you know that the testing of your faith develops perseverance. Perseverance must finish its work so that you may be mature and complete, not lacking anything (James 1:2-4).

He has given us new birth into a living hope and into an inheritance that can never perish...kept in heaven for you. In this, you greatly rejoice, though now you suffer grief in all kinds of trials. These have come so your faith...refined by fire... may be proved genuine. Though you do not see him now, you believe and are filled with inexpressible joy for you are receiving the goal of your faith, the salvation of your souls (from 1 Peter 1:3-9, authors' paraphrase).

Refining by fire is known to the modern church only as something from church history, and we rarely read our history. It's too depressing! The concept of refining is foreign to our theology, and John Bunyan's *Pilgrim's Progress* is as quaint and incomprehensible to the modern church as it is to the modern university literature class.

What a shoddy substitute is the visualized Jesus we create in our psychologized minds for the real Messiah Peter refers to. How pathetic is the peace offered by our visualization techniques that flip us onto a fluffy bird for a ride to the beach whenever we feel pain approaching! People must know that these magician's tricks are not true science, but "science" is so much more acceptable a term than is "magic."

We are told that Jesus was "...made like his brothers in every way, in order that he might become a merciful and faithful high priest in service to God, and that he might make atonement for the sins of the people. Because he himself suffered when he was tempted, he is able to help those who are being tempted" (Hebrews 2:17,18).

"During the days of Jesus' life on earth, he offered up prayers and petitions with loud cries and tears to the one who could save him from death, and he was heard because of his reverent submission. Although he was a son, he learned obedience from what he suffered" (Hebrews 5:7,8).

"I want to know Christ and the power of his resurrection and the fellowship of sharing in his sufferings..." (Philippians 3:10).

We are intensely interested in sharing in Christ's power via our "power encounter" techniques and our political organization. But sharing His suffering? Isn't that masochistic? How quaint are those verses about cries, tears, obedience, suffering, and reverent submission! Isn't it wonderful that now we have hypnosis, corrective reliving techniques, and positive confessions so we don't have to experience all that?

A friend told us recently that he didn't see the movie *Schindler's List* because he didn't feel it was "healthy" for him. He felt he would have trouble forgetting the scenes of horror. This is a man who wants to please God and does not recognize to what extent the psychological mindset and terminology is changing his theology. Seeing *Schindler's List* may not be God's will for him, but as a Christian he certainly should not base his decision on his "health." What if God wanted him to remember the scenes of horror? What if the pain of it all was meant to drive him to his knees for the Lord to mature him further? What has the church come to when our decisions revolve around what will keep us "healthy"?

Our problem is unbelief. The truths of Scripture are of no value, if we do not believe them and cling to them by faith. Moses persevered because he saw Him who was invisible (Hebrews 11:27).

"The message they heard was of no value to them, because those who heard did not combine it with faith" (Hebrews 4:2). But we want relief now. We ask, "Why isn't God doing anything about my hard times?"

We live in a moral universe created by a just God. Judgment is not without purpose. For those truly abused, for those who truly are victims, and for all the rest of us for whom life has not been "fair," the Bible holds the answer.

> And will not God bring about justice for his chosen ones, who cry out to him day and night? . . . He will see that they get justice, and quickly. However, when the Son of Man comes, will he find faith on the earth? (Luke 18:6-8).

It is mine to avenge; I will repay.... No one can deliver out of my hand.... As surely as I live forever, when I sharpen my flashing sword and my hand grasps it in judgment, I will take vengeance... and repay (Deuteronomy 32:35,39-42).

God's judgment is right, and as a result you will be counted worthy of the kingdom of God, for which you are suffering. God is just: He will pay back trouble to those who trouble you and give relief to you who are troubled.... This will happen when the Lord Jesus is revealed from heaven in blazing fire with his powerful angels (2 Thessalonians 1:5-7).

We need to remember that when the saints in Revelation 6 cried out, "How long, Sovereign Lord, holy and true, until you judge... and avenge?" they were told to wait a little longer. We need to review the Scripture passages on judgment, remind ourselves of who the real God is, and with heart pounding and lips quivering like Habakkuk, we need to say with him: "Though the fig tree does not bud and there are no grapes on the vines, though the olive crop fails and the fields produce no food, though there are no sheep in the pen and no cattle in the stalls, yet I will rejoice in the LORD, I will be joyful in God my Savior. The Sovereign LORD is my strength; he makes my feet like the feet of a deer, he enables me to go on the heights" (Habakkuk 3:17-19).

May we be found faithful.

The Collar
(the yoke of Matthew 11:29)
by George Herbert

I struck the board and cried "No more;
I will abroad!
What? shall I ever sigh and pine?
My lines and life are free, free as the road,
Loose as the wind, as large as store.
Shall I be still in suit?
Have I no harvest but a thorn
To let me blood, and not restore
What I have lost with cordial fruit?
Sure there was wine
Before my sighs did dry it; there was corn
Before my tears did drown it.
Is the year only lost to me?
Have I no bays to crown it,
No flowers, no garlands gay? All blasted?
All wasted?
Not so, my heart; but there is fruit,
And thou hast hands.
Recover all thy sigh-blown age
On double pleasures: leave thy cold dispute
Of what is fit and not. Forsake thy cage,
Thy rope of sands,
Which petty thoughts have made, and made to thee
Good cable, to enforce and draw,
And be thy law,
While thou didst wink and wouldst not see.
Away! take heed;
I will abroad.
Call in thy death's-head there, tie up thy fears.

He that forbears
To suit and serve his need,
Deserves his load."
But as I raved and grew more fierce and wild
At every word,
Methought I heard one calling, *Child!*
And I replied, *My Lord.*

6

Pastor Bill's Multiple Lies

✦————✦

THE STORY OF THE YOUNG, HANDSOME PREACHER we'll call Pastor Bill is another that is sad but true. Interestingly, this nearly-thirty-year-old leader of a 600-plus-member suburban church in the southwest was one of the most convincing subjects we've run across. In fact, had it not been for the testimony of two of his victims, no one might ever have realized that he was able to use the Christian psychotherapeutic movement to support his deceit. He needed its shaky tenets only when he was caught red-handed and had no other way out, but we're getting ahead of our case study...

Only two elders on the board at Pastor Bill's church knew of two accusations about the pastor's moral character, and they doubted the accounts. In fact, when one woman from his former church wrote a detailed account of her seduction at his hands, they didn't even tell Bill. The chairman of the elders shared it with his most trusted friend on the board, and they agreed that they would not trouble the pastor with it or stir up any controversy over such an obviously misguided attempt at hurting a man of God.

Bill had earned their trust. He had gone from a very successful youth pastorate to a whirlwind of a success as pastor of a small church that grew quickly. His hiring as senior pastor of his current, much larger church was controversial only for a week or two. Despite the fact that everyone on the staff, from the custodian to the secretary to the Christian Education man, was older than he, Pastor Bill showed such maturity and depth in the pulpit that he quickly won over all doubters. If such accounts can be believed, he had virtually no detractors by a few months into his ministry there.

He was seminary trained, a personal soul winner, an excellent Bible teacher, a winsome preacher, and he was a hard worker. He put in long hours but still seemed to find the time to devote to his very young family. Pastor Bill was handsome and popular with all ages, always eager to call on the sick and help out on work days. And on top of all that he seemed to be a good administrator.

The two elders handled the ugly letter incident by contacting the pastor of the woman's church, Bill's old congregation. They said they did not want to embarrass the woman or come down too hard on her, but that it was the responsibility of her pastor to inform her firmly that it was unbiblical to bring an unsubstantiated charge against a servant of God. He agreed and reported later that he had confronted the woman. She admitted there had been no witnesses but had hoped that Pastor Bill would break down and admit his guilt if faced with the charge.

Her current pastor asked her if her husband could at least confirm that she had been dysfunctional or adversely affected by the alleged affair, but she pleaded with him not to tell her husband. The pastor told her that that would then have to be the end of the matter.

"What is your take on this?" the elder chairman asked the woman's pastor.

"I believe we have done the right, biblical thing. Of course, knowing Bill I'm convinced he's innocent. I must say, however, that I could not get this woman to back off her story. It didn't make sense, it was filled with inconsistencies, and their few secret meetings supposedly took place at times when Bill would have had to be a master of scheduling."

"Such as?"

"Well, one episode was supposed to have taken place between Sunday school and church."

"Enough said."

The same two elders had to deal with a charge two months later when a woman in the church complained that Pastor Bill had called on her when no one else was at home, and she was nervous and uncomfortable. She said he had asked for her husband and seemed to invite himself in even though she said she was alone. "He made some suggestive comments," she said.

"Be careful," the elder said. He admonished her with the same biblical warning that had been used on the other complainant, and she was quickly subdued.

"Well," she said resignedly, "I don't know what else to say, then. There were no witnesses, and I don't guess you want me to tell you what he said."

"Let me put it this way," the elder said, "tell me first whether this is something you have told anyone else. In other words, may I assume we are to keep this from your husband?"

"Oh, no, sir. He'd be happy to talk to you. But like I say, he wasn't there."

"You told him?"

"Of course! And he's none too happy. If I tell him this is going no further, it wouldn't surprise me if he insisted on leaving the church. I mean, he's not the type to take matters into his own hands or start a ruckus, but he knows I don't lie."

"Yet you have no witnesses, and the Scripture seems clear on that requirement."

"Uh-huh."

"I'd hate to see you folks leave. You've been in this church for a long time."

"Since I was a little girl."

"Go ahead and tell me what he said, the best you can remember it. I can't promise I'll do anything with it except to consult with a trusted spiritual friend, but I think I ought to know what you're saying he said."

"Well, it embarrasses me to be too specific," she said, "and I have to admit that a lot of this is just women's intuition. I mean, I saw the way he looked at me and I read his eyes and body language."

"Excuse me, ma'am, but isn't it safe to say you're, ah, a good bit older than he is."

"At least twelve years," she said.

"So he was flattering you."

"Let me say I was not flattered. I considered him to be in the worst taste."

"Okay. What did he say specifically?"

"He told me how impressed he was with my spiritual life, the way I interacted with my teenage children."

"Uh-huh. And?"

"And that I didn't look much older than them, that I looked good in fashionable clothes, that my husband was a lucky man, and that he frankly had always kind of had a 'thing' for older women."

The elder frowned. "I agree that if he said that, it was inappropriate."

"He also said he'd like to see me again sometime when he knew my husband would be gone long enough for us to get acquainted."

The elder squinted at her. "He said that?"

She held his gaze. "Yes, sir. You can see why my husband is upset."

"Ma'am, if I were your husband I would have punched a man in the nose for saying something like that."

"I'm sure he'd like to, but you know that's not his way. Pastor Bill would just deny it, and then where would we be?"

"I can say the same to you after this conversation."

"I understand, sir. But maybe if you get any more complaints, mine will make sense. If you don't, then maybe I made a big thing over nothing."

"But if he really says what you say he did, that was more than nothing."

"That's what I think. We probably won't be around here much longer."

"I wish you'd reconsider and give me some time on this."

"I will. My parents' funerals were in this church, you know. Our roots go deep here."

When the elder shared that news with his trusted friend, they were both concerned. Either story by itself was worthy of being ignored. There was no way to have a biblical confrontation without witnesses, and these were serious charges. "Shall we take it to the board?" the chairman asked.

"I wouldn't," the other elder said. "Let's go directly to Bill with it and see if we can nip it in the bud. If we don't get a satisfactory answer, then we'll have to move further with it. I hate to say it, but sometimes where there's smoke there's fire."

"I don't know about that," the chairman said. "But where there's smoke there had at least ought to be a fireman."

The two elders met with Pastor Bill in his office, and he welcomed them warmly. The chairman did all the talking. The pastor's beaming smile faded as he realized what was happening.

"We would not have come to you with either of these charges by themselves," the elder said. "And no one else knows at this point."

◆

The elders looked at each other. This would certainly be an impossible story to check out without hurting a lot of people and disrupting the ministry of a church.

Bill folded his hands and looked down, as if sad. He shook his head slowly. "I can't tell you how grateful I am that you have handled it this way," he said, "both of you. I praise God for your spiritual leadership. I need to ask for your complete confidence in this, because I don't want to hurt either of these ladies, about whom I care very much. I have not told anyone about them for their own sakes, but obviously you need to know. Can I have your pledge of confidence?"

Both men nodded.

"I was counseling the woman in my previous church, and she confided in me that she had had an abortion before she was married. She had never told her husband. I urged her to tell him, because God had forgiven her and she needed her husband's support to be a good mother to the children she did have. She put off telling him, and then I admit I made a serious error in judgment. I told her that if she didn't tell him, I might feel forced to. She went ballistic.

"I talked to my wife about it and she graciously and tenderly pointed out how stupid I had been to say something like that. Obviously there's no way I could break a sacred confidence. I quickly assured the woman that I would never tell her secret and that she could depend upon that promise. I did, however, urge her again to tell her husband herself.

"She appeared relieved that I had not told her husband but was not convinced that I would keep my promise if she continued to keep it from him. She told me that if I ever told him, she would deny it and accuse me of an affair with her."

"Well, that's what she's done."

"But I never told her husband."

The elders looked at each other. This would certainly be an impossible story to check out without hurting a lot of people and disrupting the ministry of a church. The chairman turned back to Pastor Bill. "And this latest accusation?"

The young pastor sighed heavily. "It's true I went to her house and that her husband was not home. I said I really wanted to see them together—you know I wanted to recommend them to run Vacation Bible School this summer but I wanted to get their okay before suggesting it to Verne [the C.E. man]. As I was turning to leave, she grabbed my sleeve and insisted I come in because she had something to show me. I told her that I really couldn't if she was alone, but she said, 'No, here, just a second, look.'

"I reluctantly followed her in and she just stood there looking into my eyes and smiling. I said, 'What? What is it?' and she said something about just wanting to get a good close look at me. The Bible says 'flee,' gentlemen, and I felt so stupid at allowing myself to get into that predicament that I turned tail and ran. When I got back to the church a phone message was waiting for me from her, but I did not return it. My guess is that she knows I could never in good conscience recommend her for any volunteer spot here, and I'm sure she's afraid I might tell someone."

"So she's beating you to the punch."

"Apparently so. I appreciate your confidence, and I'd appreciate any counsel you may have for me. I told my wife, of course, but no one else. Obviously I know enough to not let myself get dragged into the house again, and in the future I will call ahead in a situation like that, but I'm wide open to input."

"Don't you think the husband should know?" the elder said.

"A good husband wouldn't believe that, and even if she admitted the truth, she could say it was innocent kidding. It may have been, but I wasn't about to stay and find out."

"Past that, we can't think of any advice," the elder said. "Neither of us was ever good-lookin' enough to get a come-on even if we'd wanted one." They all had a good laugh and prayer, and Pastor Bill was off the hook for another few weeks.

His downfall arrived in the form of a beautiful, single woman in her mid-twenties, Lena, the younger sister of a lady who—along with her husband and children—had been members of the church for about three years. The lady was a new Christian and had witnessed to Lena to no avail. Finally, when Lena was passing through town, her sister got her to stay with her and even to attend church. "You'll just love our new pastor," she said.

Little did she know that Lena had, in fact, already loved Pastor Bill.

As Lena sat in church that Sunday morning, dressed much flashier than anyone else, she kept staring at the pastor. He was preaching on marital fidelity, the sacredness of the Christian home, and the importance of modeling a healthy marriage before your children.

"What a great-looking guy!" Lena whispered.

"Tell me about it," her sister said. "But listen. He's good."

A little later Lena leaned over and whispered, "This guy looks and sounds just like the guy who dumped me in Southern California last spring."

Lena's sister knew that story. Lena had met a dashing young guy named Mark in a singles' bar. He was witty and charming and she melted for him immediately. She saw him every afternoon and spent the nights with him at her place, though he was gone all morning every day for a week. After the last night he left her a note saying he'd had a good time. She'd never heard from him again.

That wasn't the first or last time Lena had had her heart broken, but she had really believed Mark when he spoke of their destiny, their futures together, the fireworks, the bells going off. This was the real thing. For one week. Then nothing.

"Your pastor could be his twin," she whispered. "I'm going to have to ask him if he has a brother named Mark. Only Mark had the cutest little crescent-shaped scar over his left eyebrow. Said he got it scuba diving somehow."

Lena's sister's blood ran cold. She had always noticed the pastor's scar. He had even spoken of it. Something about a wagon spill when he was a toddler, lots of blood, a few stitches, and a distinguishing mark on his face. She said nothing to Lena, hoping to steer her away from the door where the pastor stood to shake hands.

But Lena would not be deterred. She was convinced this man was a brother to her lover, and she made a beeline for the door. She stood in line staring past the heads in front of her, trying to get a good look while her sister kept encouraging her to head out another way so they could beat the rush.

Her sister finally resigned herself to the fact that Lena was going through with this, and she gave up on any chance to further share the gospel with her. When Lena saw that scar, she would know the truth, the truth that had already rocked her sister to her shoes. In fact, Lena's sister didn't even want to think about it. But here she was, in line behind her as they approached Pastor Bill. She watched both faces closely as they shook hands.

Pastor Bill betrayed nothing. He looked Lena in the eye and said it was nice to meet her. "You must be sisters."

"Yes, Mark, I'm her sister," Lena said, her face pale, her lip quivering.

"I'm sorry," the pastor said. "The name's Bill. Everybody calls me Pastor Bill."

"Okay, then, *Pastor Bill,*" Lena said with sarcasm. Bill pretended she was trying to be funny and laughed.

It was all Lena's sister could do to shake her pastor's hand and mumble a greeting. He said, "It must be great to have your sister in town. Hope she can join us again."

She forced a smile and moved on. In the car Lena asked her sister and her husband if they could talk when the kids got out. Her sister nodded. The kids scrambled for the house, their mother calling after them, "Turn the oven off!"

"What's up?" Lena's brother-in-law said.

"You don't want to know," his wife said.

"Well, maybe neither of you want to know," Lena said, "but last spring your Mr.-Marriage-and-Family pastor shared my bed for a week."

Her brother-in-law whirled around in his seat. "No way, Lena! Come off it!"

"Small world, isn't it? I'll bet he was dying this morning when I showed up in his face. You want to talk about God working in mysterious ways. How about lettin' a sleep-around preacher have a fling with the sister of somebody in his church! Ha!"

"I still don't believe it," her sister said.

"Yes, you do," Lena said. "You just don't like it. You know me well enough to know that I don't make up stuff like that. And you also know I'd remember a face, and a scar, like that. Next week I'll prove it."

"How?"

"With a picture. And the note. He signed it 'Mark,' but Sis, it was Pastor Bill."

Just over a week later, with photo and note in hand, Lena's sister and her husband mustered the courage to take the evidence to the elders. This time the chairman brought in the whole board, and they prayerfully and sadly decided that the two original elders must confront the pastor again.

Pastor Bill vehemently denied the charges, saying that the church should take a confidence vote if the elders didn't have faith in him. Yes, the handwriting looked like his, but it also looked like a lot of other people's. Yes, he shared a resemblance with the man in the picture in a bathing suit, clutching a bottle of beer, his arm around the waist of Lena's bikini-clad sister. But the guy had sunglasses on. How could you be sure? "I'm telling you, it's not me. Are you calling me a liar? This is Satan attacking our church, and I'll tell you something else: I'll see you all resign before I step down over a spurious charge."

The elder chairman spoke quietly. "I would like cool heads to prevail. We all know that a serious issue like this will be difficult to keep under wraps for long. For the sake of everyone involved, the pastor, his wife, our parishioners, the church, and supremely the reputation of Christ, I'm asking all of us to keep this in utmost confidence until we decide upon action."

"Don't leave me hanging," Pastor Bill said. "If you're going to abandon me, don't keep me in the dark. If you choose to believe lies from the pit over the man God called to be your shepherd, may He have mercy on you."

The elder chairman got little sleep that night, and he was stunned when he got a call at work the next day from the pastor's wife. She asked to meet him with his wife at his home that very afternoon. He rearranged his schedule.

He didn't know what to expect. Would she furiously defend her husband, or did she just want to know what was going on? Clearly Pastor Bill had told her he was under attack. She deserved some answers.

What developed was the worst imaginable. His wife began, "Last spring Bill was at that training institute in Southern California. They had classes every morning and were free the rest of the day. I could never reach him. Sometimes he called me at noon. He said he and the other guys played golf all afternoon and went out in.the evenings or met for prayer and Bible study. He never mentioned any names of new friends he made there. It reminded me of how hard it is to reach him whenever he's away speaking at other churches or meetings. I always felt terrible for being suspicious. Everybody loves him and he's so spiritual. Who am I to accuse him of anything?"

"Let me ask you a question," the elder said. "Do you recall his consulting you about a woman he was counseling at your previous church?"

She shook her head.

"Let me tell you a little more to see if it jogs a memory. It seems—"

"No," she interrupted, "he never counseled any women. That church didn't believe in that and he agreed. They had a group of deaconesses who handled all that."

"Well, this was a woman who came to him on her own with a problem from her past that she didn't want to tell her husband about."

"I'm sorry, I don't recall anything like that."

"He was supposed to have told her that if she didn't tell her husband, he would. Remember?"

She shook her head.

"He said he told you all about it and that you gently told him he had made a mistake."

"He told you this?"

"Yes, ma'am."

"Bill has never told me about his counseling, which I always assumed was only with men. I always admired the fact that he never told me private things about people in the church."

"So this story doesn't jibe with your memory?"

"I would have remembered this. What was this woman supposed to have done in her past?"

"Since I haven't mentioned a name, I suppose I can say what he said. It was an abortion before she was married."

———————————◆———————————

Pastor Bill exploded. "If you think I'm going to stand before this congregation and my wife and God and admit to things I did not do, you've got another thing coming!"

The pastor's wife sat there shaking her head and crying. "It could be true, I guess," she said, "but he and I never discussed anything like that."

"Let me ask you another one."

"Oh, no."

"I won't if you don't want me to."

"Go ahead."

"Did he tell you that a woman from our church invited him into her house even though her husband was not home?"

"No! Did he go in?"

"He says just briefly before he realized what she was up to and then he left immediately and told you all about it."

"Not true."

"I'm sorry."

"*You're* sorry? I'm sitting here calling your pastor and my husband a liar."

The elder chairman had one more call to make. He talked to Pastor Bill's secretary, one of the elder's oldest and dearest friends. "I wouldn't normally ask this of you, Sylvia," he said, "but I need to ask you something and ask you not to say anything to the pastor about it."

"Wow, I don't know."

"I appreciate your loyalty, dear, but I really need your help and need you to trust me."

"Well," she whispered, "he came slamming in here today saying you guys were all out to get him. Tell me it's nothing serious."

"I wish I could. All I need to know is the phone log." He told her he wanted a quick rundown of who called the pastor on the date Bill said he had been enticed into the woman's house. Sylvia read off the list of calls. None were from the woman, making a lie his account of a phone message waiting from her when he got back to the office.

That night the elders met in emergency session and then called Pastor Bill to join them. They told him they felt before God that the charges against him were true. He was given an option. If he would voluntarily step down, the church would support him and his family temporarily, pay for his counseling, and begin discipline procedures that could eventually restore him to fellowship, if not to the pastorate.

Pastor Bill exploded. "If you think I'm going to stand before this congregation and my wife and God and admit to things I did not do, you've got another thing coming! A brother isn't supposed to sue a brother, but if you follow through with this and let me down, I'll have to conclude that you are not my brothers, and you'll have a defamation suit on your hands. You're about to ruin reputations, ministries, families."

The elder chairman was not cowed. "Bill, you can step down and humbly accept our offer, or we will announce your termination and explain the reasons to the congregation ourselves. Legal action is up to you, but you will not stand in the pulpit of this church again."

Bill asked for and was granted twenty-four hours to think it over. He came to the elder chairman alone and in tears. His voice was thick with emotion. "I want you to just listen to me. First, I swear on the Bible and on the lives of my wife and children that I am innocent. God has told me not to sue you, so I won't. I will step down for personal reasons, but I will confess nothing, because I did nothing. I will agree to counseling, but I want your assurance that if the counselor determines that I have been wrongly accused, I will be exonerated and reinstated."

The elder sat, shoulders slumped. He was relieved and troubled. There would be no ugly fight, at least not soon. "You know rumors will fly."

"I know. But if I'm not confessing and the board is not talking, I believe people will give me the benefit of the doubt."

"You will not be allowed in the pulpit to defend yourself during this process."

"Fair enough. But this will give me time to prove my innocence."

The elder agreed and went to the local seminary to talk to the chief of the counseling department, who would take the case himself. "Is it possible, in the face of all this evidence, that the man is innocent?" the elder asked. "I mean, what was all this swearing on the lives of his family? That's pretty severe stuff."

The counselor smiled. "You see the kind of a position we always find ourselves in? The innocent man would say that, wouldn't he? Unfortunately, so would most guilty men."

Bill went for counseling. Meanwhile, the issue nearly destroyed the church. Parishioners demanded a meeting with the board. They wanted details. No one would believe the charges that were rumored, and the board had agreed they would not discuss them until after there was some resolution in the counseling. Some called for the resignation of the board, others were not satisfied with any substitute in the pulpit. Until Bill would confess publicly, the problem would rage.

The biggest problem, however, was what was happening behind closed doors in the counseling sessions. Bill resolutely maintained his innocence in the face of damning evidence. Meanwhile, more women were coming forward with what they had thought were isolated incidents of indiscretions. Some came from college or seminary classmates, some from women in his former church, one from a teenager.

The board didn't know if this was just a shark feeding frenzy on a bleeding reputation or if they had a problem on their hands worse than they had ever dreamed. Even the counselor had to admit: the man was guilty. Why was he still so resolute in his denials?

7

Pastor Bill's Multiple Lives
Multiple Personality Disorder: Invented Irresponsibility

◆————◆

D R. DON CORNELL, THE WIDELY PUBLISHED and re-spected head of counseling at the local seminary, found Bill a difficult client. Don had been aware of Pastor Bill for quite some time, having heard him speak at chapel twice in the last six months and noting with interest his fast rise within his denomination. He was saddened by the charges brought against the young man, but when he saw all the evidence, it was clear to him—as to anyone in his right mind—that Bill had indeed been living a double life.

Dr. Cornell had started with a fatherly approach, gently trying to get Bill to see that he was in deep trouble. "Deep trouble?" Bill responded. "This is Kafkaesque! I know my anger makes me look guilty and I know all my denial looks like just that. But let me tell you, I am innocent and I am angry and I feel betrayed. My board has let me down. They have believed false reports.

I have not been given the benefit of the doubt. I have not been given due process. I thought I could count on my wife's support, but she has apparently turned against me."

"Oh, but she's standing with you all the way," Dr. Cornell said.

"She hasn't left me, you mean. Who knows what she's told the children?"

"Nothing, she says. They're too young."

"But I can see it in them. They know."

"Well, they may know something's wrong. Daddy's not preaching anymore, not going to work, he's out of sorts, but surely you don't think she's told them sordid details—"

"I'm not sure of anything anymore, but I want you to know right off the bat, I need you as an ally. I have no one else. And I want you to believe me. I'm innocent."

Dr. Cornell had faced some tough cases, but this man was entrenched. He had to keep reminding himself, *I've seen the evidence. The man is guilty.* Apparently Bill was looking for some expression of support, and the therapist was not able to offer it—at least not on this matter of guilt or innocence. He didn't want to set Bill back even further, so he changed the subject to get closer to the answer he needed most: This posture was so vehement, so convincing that it could be one of only two things— massive denial or flat-out lying.

When Dr. Cornell asked Bill to tell him his history, he was amazed to see the young man immediately warm to the subject. Gone was the desperate, forlorn look. He displayed an excellent memory and described in detail a very normal, happy childhood, the son of a pastor. He was the oldest of three children, none of whom "went off the deep end," as he put it. He was a model child and teen, often dubbed "a perfect angel."

The story of college and seminary—athlete with good grades, meeting his wife, student body president—was straightforward. Whenever there was a lull in the conversation, Bill clouded over, as if remembering his plight. "I'm innocent, Doctor," he would say. "Can't you convince the board?"

But Dr. Cornell was not convinced himself. *Such massive denial,* he thought. *Who can be that good, that consistent? There must be something he's not telling me.* "We have a lot of work ahead of us," he told Bill cryptically.

Over the next several weeks, he probed different areas. "I notice that one of the women making a charge against you said you had had a week-long affair with her."

"Never saw her before in my life."

"Has that ever happened to you before?"

"An affair? Absolutely not!"

"No, I mean someone claiming they had met you before and your having no knowledge of them."

Bill appeared to think for a moment. "No," he said uncertainly. "Well—no, I don't think so."

"Take your time."

"Well, that happens to everyone once in a while, doesn't it? Being mistaken for someone else, I mean."

"Sure, but it's disconcerting when someone is so insistent. If I told someone that they must have me mixed up with someone else and they kept pushing, it would make me wonder if I was wrong."

"Well, I wasn't wrong. I never saw that woman—"
He paused.

"Yes? What is it?"

"Well, I do have a vague recollection of that happening to me before. It was in seminary."

___

"What happened?"

"The wife of a classmate of mine worked in a convenience store. When he introduced her to me at a get-together, she said she had waited on me a couple of nights before. I told her I had never been to that store, but she was so sure. She kept saying, 'No, remember? Remember? You only had a twenty and it came to like five-oh-something and you kept digging for change." I didn't have any idea what she was talking about and so I just kept denying it. She kinda got upset at me because she was so sure. She told me what kind of sweatshirt and cap I was wearing, both from the same college, but I told her I never wear a hat."

"Interesting. Did you doubt yourself?"

"Only when she said the name of the college and it was the one I graduated from. But she must have known that from her husband."

"Is that it?"

"Well, it was kind of funny because the next day he told me privately that if I was going to buy a girlie magazine in that town, I ought to go to another store or wear a better disguise."

"His wife told him you bought pornography?"

"I guess."

"Is that a problem for you?"

"What?"

"Porn."

"No. I admit I've seen some and, sure, it might be a temptation, but I wouldn't buy it, no."

"This girl didn't identify you by your scar, like the other one, did she?"

"No, well, I was wearing a cap. I mean, this guy she's talking about was wearing a cap, so I don't guess that would have shown anyway."

"Would you say you have a rich fantasy life?"

"Depends on how you're defining it. Are we back on pornography again?"

"We're back on whatever you want to talk about."

"Well, yeah, I can, I have fantasized. My wife and I have a good sex life, if that's what you mean. And when I did look at porn, I mean when I was younger and all that, yeah, I could lose myself in my fantasies."

"So, how did that square with your image as the perfect adolescent?"

"I felt pretty guilty a lot of the time."

"What did you do about that?"

"Prayed, resolved, started over. I was pretty frustrated until I learned to flee instead of standing and fighting temptation."

"That's a good biblical approach. Listen, I recall from your speaking at chapel here that you were quite a storyteller. Some of your anecdotes were true, but others you seem to have made up to make a point, and they were very entertaining."

"Thank you."

"Do you often daydream such stories, making up things?"

Bill seemed to think for a moment. "Yeah, I've done that all my life."

Deciding to abruptly turn a corner, Dr. Cornell tried a surprising question. "Have you ever lost track of time?"

"How do you mean? Preached too long? Sure."

"No, I mean where you might lose yourself in your daydreams or fantasies or stories and not be conscious of where you are or what you're doing."

Bill nodded. "That happens. Nothing serious. But I can drive home and forget passing the usual spots, wondering how I got to the driveway without thinking about it. That happens to everybody, though, doesn't it? Especially when you travel the same route every day?"

"Did that ever get you in trouble?"

"When I was a teen-ager, yeah. Sometimes I'd do the dumbest things that weren't at all like me."

"So you weren't always seen as the perfect angel?"

"Not when I did something stupid, like forget I was supposed to be going to the store for my mother and ending up playing a couple of hours of basketball and going home empty-handed."

Dr. Cornell thought long and hard about what was gradually coming out about Bill. And he was impressed that his client still steadfastly maintained his innocence. He became convinced that Bill was not lying. Who could be that earnest in the face of such evidence? Bill had to somehow be unaware of his double life.

At their next session, Don Cornell proffered a theory. "It's very possible," he said, "that you were unaware of the burden of pressure placed on you to be a model child. Your mind tried to resist by creating your own little worlds and escaping into them at times. Who knows what you did when you lost track of time or did things that didn't seem like you at all? It's conceivable that you escaped into other personalities who did things your conscious mind was unaware of."

"You're talking about Multiple Personality Disorder? I've read about that. I didn't think that was a real disease."

Dr. Cornell was peeved, but he controlled himself. He set about educating Bill about M.P.D. "At minimum, you suffered emotional abuse at the hands of your super-straitlaced parents. Whereas you first escaped the confines of this kind of a life through fantasies and daydreams, beneath the facade of 'the perfect angel' lurked a growing 'other self' that yearned to express itself. That other self, seeking fun and freedom, could not reveal itself for fear of shame and punishment. It had to express itself in fantasy and then later in the form of an alter personality."

Bill laughed. "You've got to be kidding!"

Dr. Cornell leaned forward, not smiling. "Bill, I'm trying to help you. If you don't trust me or if you resist what my experience and training leads me to postulate, it ties my hands. You may have been an excellent student and pastor, but do you really feel qualified to sit there and question the facts, the authority of my discipline, the scientific research that backs me, not to mention my own reputation?"

"Well, I'm sorry if I have offended you, Doctor, but you can imagine how this sounds to me. Now you're telling me that I did all these things but I didn't know it?"

"You can choose to resist this approach if you wish," the therapist said. "But you're throwing out the one hope of putting the blame where it really belongs—on the alter personality and the abuse that caused it to rise up. Otherwise, if you're guilty, you're lying and there is no cure or restoration to ministry."

"But if I really have M.P.D., I can be cured?"

"I've seen amazing results."

"And restored?"

"That's out of my purview, but M.P.D. would certainly explain the consistent denials. My guess is that your Bill personality would pass a lie detector test. You really believe you didn't commit these acts."

"That's right."

"And yet someone in your body did. That's clear."

"It's not clear to me."

To cut through the defenses and the denial, Dr. Cornell recommended hypnosis. That was so the usual control over Bill's mind would be suspended and "truth" could be revealed. By now Bill was an eager participant. He relaxed easily as he went under hypnosis and the doctor carefully asked questions and waited for answers indicating the presence of an alter. When answers were not forthcoming, he made gentle suggestions, gradually prodding and occasionally praising Bill when his responses were closer to what he was seeking. Suddenly, "Bob" emerged.

Bob was another person living inside of Bill. He used Bill's body and voice, but his manners and morals were decidedly the opposite of Bill's. He was bawdy, seductive, a jokester, ribald, and rowdy. He recounted sexual escapades and laughed about getting away with them. He even talked conspiratorially about keeping all this from Bill.

Bill was lying. His wife knew it. His board knew it. She and they felt that this diagnosis kept Bill from taking responsibility for his own sin.

Long hours were spent soliciting the graphic details of numerous affairs and close calls. Bob seemed to enjoy the telling, just as the therapist invited more and more to be revealed. Next came the job of integrating the two divergent personalities so that Bill, the "host," could achieve a "healthier self" and be comfortable with his total personality. The passively abusive parenting had to be fully exposed and understood for what it was (the cause of all of Bill's—and Bob's—problems). Anger at his parents and perhaps at God Himself must be expressed and lived out so that the energy behind the neurotic perfect angel and the debaucher could be melded and manifested in a new, integrated, whole person.

What Dr. Cornell knew but did not reveal to Bill was that this new self would contain a good deal of both personalities, now free to express themselves. He would have a wider repertoire of behaviors because he would have integrated his bad side into his consciousness.

Suddenly Bill—and Bob—became the perfect client. He jumped into this with a vengeance, eager to blame his sordid activity on his alter ego. The problem was, of course, that Bill was lying, just as he had lied about the first two accusations and about the fact that he had told his wife about the encounters. His wife knew it. His board knew it. She and they felt that this diagnosis kept Bill from taking responsibility for his own sin.

She didn't like the new freedom of expression that his therapy had afforded him. Worst of all, in Bill's mind, was that she was convinced he was not ready to return to the pastorate. "Maybe a year or two after you have made a public confession and submit to real discipline," she said. The board also said it had never seen any real conviction of sin and repentance, for which they had prayed.

Yet Bill received offers from many churches. They knew he had been through "rough times," but he had the full endorsement of a renowned therapist at a seminary, and they were willing to take a chance—even after he divorced his wife and remarried.

He is in another pastorate today, enjoying his ministry and his "healthier" self. If two of his former victims had witnesses, they could do him in because of the fact that during his therapy he called and laughed with them about how he had gotten away with it. Of course, even the calls were blamed on Bob, and who would believe isolated, unsubstantiated testimony anyway?

Multiple Personality Disorder: Invented Irresponsibility

The National Aeronautics and Space Administration (NASA) has embarked on a ten-year effort to search for intelligent life elsewhere in the universe. It plans to spend $100 million on a "High Resolution Microwave Survey," formerly called "Search for Extra-Terrestrial Intelligence." The effort bases any chance of success on the presumption that other life-forms have discovered the same scientific truths as we here on earth, and thus could understand and respond to our signals.

As you might expect, there is much debate in scientific circles over the merits of this venture. John D. Barrow, an astronomer, explores the issue of whether something we know, like mathematics or physics, is "discovered" or "invented." Is what we know something that is true universally and eternally for all to discover, or does it seem true only because of the way in which we look at it or think about it?[1]

To discover is to obtain knowledge by search and study, to reveal, to expose, to uncover, to be the first to find. To invent is to conceive of or devise, to originate, to fabricate, to make up. The dictionary makes a distinction between these two terms. For a scientist like Barrow, the difference between the two endeavors is of fundamental importance.

Was insight-oriented or depth psychotherapy discovered or invented? The answer is the difference between truth and error and is thus of fundamental importance in our critical assessment of the psychotherapy industry.

For many years Einstein was appropriately credited with the *invention* of Relativity. Only after it was possible to test his theory was he then credited with the *discovery* of Relativity. Alarmingly, the field of psychotherapy sees little or no need to rigorously test its theories, conclusions, or propositions. It merely assumes discoveries of universal truths and seems never to consider that they might be mere inventions.

No phenomenon in the history of the psychotherapy movement demonstrates more the need to discriminate between discovery and invention than the exciting, so-called Multiple Personality Disorder. At present, M.P.D. is the runaway best-seller of psychiatric diagnoses. Cases are popping up all over; numerous articles, both lay and professional, are published each year on the subject. Therapists everywhere are elated when they come upon a case, and there is no little pride in the number of different personalities (alters) the therapist is able to find in the patient.

Much of the increased prevalence of M.P.D. is due to a recently heightened interest in the long-claimed association between M.P.D. and early-life abuse.[2] In a recent survey, the National Institute of Mental Health reported that 97% of M.P.D. cases reported significant childhood trauma, generally beginning before the age of five.[3] This claim of early-life abuse has assumed so much importance in M.P.D. (as well as everywhere else in our culture) that the concept has developed recently that M.P.D. is really a kind of "Post-Traumatic Stress Disorder (P.T.S.D.)."

As many as 80% of M.P.D. sufferers are said to qualify for the P.T.S.D. diagnosis.[4] There are now a reported three million M.P.D. sufferers in America, a figure based on the assumed statistical association between the accepted high frequency of child abuse and the belief that at least 1% of these cases will manifest M.P.D. as adults.[5]

Some 90% of reported M.P.D. cases are female.[6] Those diagnosed as M.P.D. have long been known to have a host of other psychiatric diagnoses and have typically been involved in the psychotherapy system for many years.[7] Finally, we should note that the M.P.D. diagnosis "has many supporters in North America but is viewed with skepticism by others and is rarely, if ever, found in Japan . . . or Britain."[8,9,10]

Is M.P.D. a valid syndrome? Is it a real entity? When cases are found, does it represent discovery of a true disease, or is it just another invention of the psychotherapy industry? Some psychological authors are critical of their peers who accept the notion of M.P.D.[11] and believe it is grossly overdiagnosed.[12] However, the industry moves blithely onward, searching for memories, signs, and symptoms, collecting and connecting, placing the patients into groupings like M.P.D., P.T.S.D., or Adult Victim.

M.P.D. has a history as long as the psychotherapy movement itself; its popularity has waxed and waned in the same way that so many fads and "schools" in the movement have done. The first case description to later come to be called M.P.D. was Mary Reynold in 1816.[13] The report of that Pennsylvania woman was sketchy and not firsthand.

Over the ensuing decades sporadic cases were reported. In 1876, a collection of these few cases was published.[14] Following that book's dissemination, a number of new cases were reported. Most of these came from France at a time of resurgence of interest in altered states of consciousness like "dissociation" and hypnosis.

Interest in M.P.D. waned, however, until 1908 when another review of the subject was published.[15] This publication was followed again by increased numbers of new cases. Both interest and incidence declined until 1957 when *The Three Faces of Eve* was published, with its popular film version soon following.[16] From that point, the M.P.D. phenomenon has mushroomed —but only in America. Since then, many therapists unquestioningly have accepted M.P.D. as a valid syndrome. A Christian psychotherapist reports that he has led to Christ three of the five personalities in a client, and a 27-year-old waitress in Oshkosh, Wisconsin, had 6 of her 46 personalities sworn in to give testimony in court![17]

Throughout its up-and-down history, however, M.P.D. has raised eyebrows of disbelief and has never been universally accepted. Its incidence has always been in direct proportion to the public or professional notoriety attached to it. Not until 1987 did the American Psychiatric Association make a place for it in its Diagnostic and Statistical Manual (the same manual from which homosexuality was excluded by vote).

More recently, careful reviews of case reports have failed to establish M.P.D. as a valid syndrome.

One more recent review of the subject exhaustively studied prominent cases from America and Europe, looking for psychiatric conditions with which M.P.D. might be confused or for conditions that might promote it. This review also studied the way in which the second personality emerged. The report concludes: "no case has been found in which M.P.D. as now conceived is proven to have emerged through unconscious processes without any shaping or preparation by external factors such as physicians or the media."[18] That same report goes on to say that "M.P.D. never occurs as a spontaneous persistent natural event in adults...suggestion, social encouragement, preparation by expectation, and the reward of attention can produce and sustain a second personality."

That author is not alone in his conclusion that M.P.D. is a concoction of the psychotherapy industry. There is concern among many professionals that opting for an M.P.D. diagnosis may actually deny proper and effective treatment for what may be other valid, treatable conditions. Real illness may be missed by packaging the patient's problems into the provocative but tenuous diagnosis called M.P.D.

Some people are more naive and suggestible than others. Some would like to be somebody else. Some have vivid capacities for imagination and can lose themselves in their thoughts, dreams, and fantasies. Others can escape in these ways at will while others do so only in the face of stress or upset.

These human traits or capacities have been studied by scientists since the middle of the last century. They are described by terms such as "dissociation" and "hypnotizability." Those terms, like so many in psychology, are really metaphors or descriptors of who we are as human beings, as well as what we do. Beyond their use to describe, such terms have little meaning. In spite of the very tentative nature of the meaning of "dissociation," most psychological authors use it in anything but a tentative way.[19]

Entire theories are built on such terms, ideas, and metaphors, which are anything but solid, tested, or proven. Unfortunately, the entire psychotherapy industry, its theories, and its practices rest on colorful, intriguing metaphors.

To take human traits and capacities and assemble them into a tantalizing "disorder" may be the stuff of novels and movies, but is a diagnosis such as M.P.D. of real service to mankind? To make M.P.D. a psychiatric diagnosis is to place emphasis on a symptom. Almost invariably, such a symptom is a means by which the person is dealing with the trials of life in a manner outside God's will. It provides a path of escape or denial, which is never God's will for us, as He promised never to test us beyond what we can bear.

Symptoms we see described in M.P.D. are not unexpected in a fallen race, but they are a result of failure to choose biblical solutions. It is a disservice to the sufferer to label as a disease his tactic of escape, denial, and avoidance. How much better it would be to give attention to the heart, which lies at the root of the avoidance, than to place the attention on the fascinating symptoms!

It is best to deny preoccupation with an altered personality state, to deprive it of the attention that nurtures it, and to focus on what the Bible teaches and what God rewards: faith, obedience, and perseverance.

8

Edith's Empty Love Tank

◆————————◆

A S THIS CASE STUDY is personally closer to us than the others, we have taken the liberty of adjusting even more details than normal to make it impossible for anyone to identify the principals. We are pleased to say that this story is one of those few that has a happy ending. Sadly, that cannot be said for so many victims who see psychotherapy—including Christian psychotherapy—as the answer to their problems.

Just before the trouble began, Edith was a functioning Christian wife and mother, quite content with her lot in life. She had gone from Christian high school to Christian college, and met her future husband, Bruce, the first week on campus. Edith studied education with plans to be a schoolteacher, but she and Bruce were married the month after graduation (he became an accountant and would provide a comfortable life for them), and she was soon pregnant with the first of their two boys. Edith happily set aside her career goal, agree-ing with Bruce that she should play a traditional role at home while her kids were young.

The older son, Jeff, was a great kid, getting good grades, making lots of friends, and enjoying church. Edith and Bruce raised him and his little brother the way they were raised, conservatively, biblically, and with lots of interaction and fun. They were a close family.

When Jeff became a senior at the local Christian high school (his younger brother was in eighth grade), Edith began working part time in real estate sales so they could put aside a little money for his college education. She enjoyed learning the business and getting out into the workaday world, happy that she didn't have to study as much or put in the hours of the full-time Realtors. That would require too much time away from home, and her family priorities were still intact.

The first time Jeff got into any kind of trouble was the Sunday he was found waiting for them in the car at the end of church. The high school group had their own services, but he had been booted out and was told to go sit with his parents in church if he couldn't behave. He had stormed out and was sitting behind the wheel of the family car when they got out of church. Normally they had to wait for him.

His parents asked innocently what was up, and he angrily reported that he had been treated like a junior higher. "If they want to kick me out, they can kick me out, but they're not making me sit with Mommy and Daddy!"

Normally Edith was able to get Jeff to tell her any-thing, but she could not drag out of him what had caused the commotion. All he would say was, "I was just kidding around. No big deal."

"Well, apparently it was a big enough deal to your teacher. If you won't tell me, I'll ask him."

"Now *you're* treating me like a child! I'm almost 18!"

"Then start acting like it. You know better than to do something that will get you kicked out of high school church. Your father and I have been active in this church for twenty years. One more incident like this and I'll go to your teacher."

That solved whatever the crisis had been at church, but the next week Edith had to let another Realtor take over on a viewing because she was called into the guidance counselor's office at school. What now?

There she learned the shocking news that Jeff's grades were declining in every subject. "I thought you'd want to know before midterm grades come home." She appreciated it and asked what the guidance counselor thought was the problem. "That's just it. I was hoping you could tell me. Jeff's teachers say he's becoming a smart aleck and disruptive, trying to be funny at inappropriate times. He's not doing well on homework. You know we expected him to be in the top five in the class, but he's quickly sliding. Anything wrong at home?"

Edith told the church story, but said that had cleared up with her threat to go to the teacher.

"Maybe you need to do the same here," he said.

"He really hated that idea. I just don't understand it."

"I'm worried too that Jeff has not yet committed to a college," the guidance counselor said.

"I know. He won't even tell us whether he's going to college at all. I'm working to help pay for it, but he's saying he might just want to work. I'd hate to see him do that, unless he needs a year to grow up a little. I wouldn't have thought he needed that until now."

"Some kids, especially boys, hate the idea of growing up," the counselor said. "College sounds very adult, and they realize that this is it. They're men now. What they don't realize is that college is fun and can be the highlight of their lives."

"Believe me, we've tried to tell him that." She sighed. "What happened to our trouble-free boy? We never expected any hassle out of Jeff. At least he's not into anything bad like drugs or alcohol."

"Yeah, I think that's clear. We can usually tell, and there hasn't been that kind of trouble here for several years. I was wondering, do you think there would be value in Jeff's going for some counseling? I mean, something's clearly going on in his life, and maybe he's just not comfortable telling you and your husband. Maybe he'd open up to someone else."

"How about you?"

"Oh, I don't think so. I've been his class sponsor and we've been close over the years. I kind of have the feeling that he would see me as a parental figure too. We recommend a Christian counseling center associated with a local church. Lots of kids here have benefited."

Jeff was outraged. It was all Edith and Bruce could do to get him to go. Edith told him it was either that or she would go with him to talk to each and every one of his teachers to find out what they thought was the problem. "I don't have a problem, Mom," he said. "I've just been goofing off."

"Well, your guidance counselor thinks it's more than that, so you'll keep this appointment."

Jeff's therapist, Dr. Finch, was met by one furious young man. Jeff told him in no uncertain terms that he was not crazy, that he did not need a shrink, and that if his parents insisted on this he was going to run away. He spent the rest of the time with his hands thrust deep into his pockets, slouching, and staring everywhere but at

Dr. Finch. By the time Jeff got home, Dr. Finch had called and reported the news to Edith.

She and Bruce were shocked. They didn't want to do anything that would cause Jeff to bolt, but they were determined to get to the bottom of his problem. "Let me ask you one thing, ma'am," Dr. Finch said. "Did you tell your son he had to straighten up in church because you and your husband's reputations were on the line?"

Edith racked her brain. Had that been what she said? "I may have," she said. "It was in the heat of the moment and my point was that he knew better."

"Well, you let me know what you want to do about his coming back. I'll be happy to see him, but we might make more progress if I could see you."

"I'll do whatever you think is best," she said. "I'll be happy to come."

Jeff was thrilled with that news. "I promise I'll do better at school if I don't have to go back and face all those weird questions from that Finch guy. No more screwing around, and I'll get back on track with my grades."

"It's a deal," Edith said. "But I'm going to work with Dr. Finch on whatever he feels is the best way to motivate you."

"Great. As long as I don't have to be there."

The following week Edith took Jeff's high school transcripts, achievement test scores, and teacher evaluations to her appointment with Dr. Finch. "Frankly," she told him, "I'm worried. He promised to do better, but I feel like a worthless mother, and I need some help to get through this mess."

"Let's talk about you and that feeling," Dr. Finch said.

"Well, I'd really rather talk about Jeff."

"Oh, we will. But I need to know as much as I can about the family dynamic, structure, and function so I can make meaningful recommendations. Even after one session with Jeff I can tell there are deeper problems there than he is ready to face. I found him unwilling to answer any questions that even bordered on the personal. That concerns me."

Dr. Finch had concluded by saying that next time he wanted to delve more deeply into "what was really going on in the life of this supposedly normal and fulfilled woman."

Edith was alarmed. *What is wrong with my son?* she wondered. She resolved to do whatever the therapist recommended and became a willing and eager participant in the process. She would be whatever Jeff was unwilling to be in this endeavor. She would even answer the tough, personal questions, if Dr. Finch thought that would be of value.

His first goal was to know her history. Edith found it fun and interesting to recount her life story for someone. She kept admitting that it was boring and that she had never really been anywhere or done anything exciting, but she insisted she was happy and fulfilled as a wife and mother and active, churchgoing Christian. "Before this little ripple with Jeff, I would have said I had the perfect life," she said.

When she got home she told Bruce how exhilarating it had been and that he should come with her and get involved. "One patient in the family is enough at one time," he said. "I'm glad both you and Jeff aren't going at the same time or I'd have to go just to defend myself."

Edith withheld from her husband one troubling aspect of that first session. Dr. Finch had concluded by saying that next time he wanted to delve more deeply into "what was really going on in the life of this supposedly normal and fulfilled woman whose son obviously had some deep-seated problems."

Edith derived from that that she may have been right about feeling like a worthless mother. He had not countered her statement about that, and yet wasn't that the role of these therapists? To let a person speak her mind and discover her own truths about herself? She had said that, only hoping that he would reassure her she was okay. Was there something wrong with her that manifested itself in her son? If there was, she wanted to know so she could deal with it, root it out, and return to being for her son all he needed her to be. She was, after all, first and foremost a wife and mother. That, she felt, was her role in life, and she loved it.

The next week, Dr. Finch told Edith that what was most important to him in helping evaluate the family situation was her feelings.

"My feelings?"

"Yes. I need to explore your emotions, your frame of mind about the facts of your life, not just your thoughts or conclusions. You have given me a rather detailed history of your life," he said, riffling through his notes. "But you haven't told me how you feel about all this."

"Well, I told you I'm upset and feel like a failure because of whatever Jeff's going through. He had a much better week at school, by the way."

"I must have really scared him off! Well, that's good, but I need to know how you feel about the course of your life."

Edith bit her lip and shrugged. "Well, I guess I feel okay. I mean, I'm happy. I love my husband and my kids and my church. No complaints, really."

Dr. Finch pursed his lips and stroked his chin, clearly frustrated. "Have you noticed that when I ask for your feelings, you generally wind up telling me about your activities, your roles, and the other people in your life?"

"Well, I'm sorry. I'm trying. They *are* my life."

"I'm sure they are, but how do you feel about that?"

Edith realized she was not being productive. Suddenly she felt very pedestrian and uneducated. Evidently she was not in tune with how psychologists worked and what they needed. She wasn't a modern woman, an up-to-date thinker. She was not in the habit of dwelling on her feelings, as opposed to being devoted to others' needs. She realized she had not answered his question and she looked pleadingly at him, as if she would like to help but didn't know how.

"Let me see if I can assist you in this," Dr. Finch said. "I want to ask you more specific questions to give you an idea what I'm trying to get at. Once we get your engine running, you can take off from there."

She brightened. "Sort of a jump start for the brain?"

"Exactly. Let's start with your own self-image, your self-esteem. Would you say you're the woman you always hoped you would be?"

"You mean character-wise? I guess, yes."

"In all ways. Are you the person you always wanted to be?"

"Well, I guess I always wanted to have the character of my parents, but that's a pretty lofty goal. They're very

148

special people and outstanding Christians. I'd be happy to have half their character."

"And do you?"

"I'm working on it through my daily devotions and prayer life and Bible study at church."

"And how do you feel about that?"

"There you go again with the tough questions." She smiled. "I guess I feel like I'm getting there."

Dr. Finch stood and paced, and Edith felt as if she was still floundering. "Let me suggest to you what I'm hearing," he said. "There is evidence here of a lack of self-esteem."

"Well, hey, I'm a sinner."

"We're all sinners, but I don't believe God would have us suffering from low self-images, do you? I mean, we were good enough for Him."

"Yeah, okay."

"You don't sound convinced."

"I'm following you. I think I feel pretty good about my relationship with the Lord."

"Edith, let me suggest that every relationship you have is with a lord of some sort."

"I'm sorry?"

"You have a relationship with God in which you rightfully feel like the inferior partner, am I right?"

"Of course. He's perfect and infinite."

"And you're finite and imperfect. Fine. But you serve your church. You serve your kids. You serve your husband. You serve your boss. You serve your college fund."

"Well," she said, "what did the pop song say? 'You gotta serve somebody.' We all do. You have bosses and responsibilities. So do I. It's my whole life. My responsibilities give me structure."

Edith wasn't sure where that came from. She thought her answer sounded fairly articulate, even psychological. But it was plain that Dr. Finch was still fishing for something.

"Isn't it fair to say that you sacrificed your teaching dream to be a housewife?"

"I wouldn't word it that way, but yes. I did it willingly. I'd rather be what I am than a career woman. It's more fulfilling."

"Well, you're starting to express your feelings, but I'm not sure I believe you."

Edith was getting steamed. She wanted to be helpful. She wanted this to work. But she had come here to help her son get back on track, and now she was playing mumbo-jumbo tug-of-war with a counselor who obviously knew what he wanted to hear. She was tempted to say, "Why don't you just tell me how I'm feeling?" but she held her tongue.

"I'm not calling you a liar," he said. "I just wonder if you're in touch with the truth of your inner feelings. Is it really more fulfilling to be in a subservient role in every area of your life than it would be to be in a profession where you mold lives, make money, get positive strokes? Do you get rewarded for all you do for your family?"

"I think they appreciate it."

"You *think?* Do they really understand all you do? Do they have any idea the hours, the effort, the unending tasks?"

Edith had to admit there were times when she wondered if anybody but she cared whether the house was clean, the laundry done, the dishes washed. She could use a few more compliments and a lot more help, sure. Who couldn't? On the other hand, she wasn't sure she expressed enough appreciation for what Bruce did for *her* either. It was give and take. The kids were ungrateful, but so had she been as a child. They would grow up and get married and have kids and come to the shocking realization how much their parents loved them and did for them, just like she did. She lived for that first letter from her newlywed kids, when they realized how much she meant to them. She had written a letter like that.

In subsequent sessions Dr. Finch walked her through her childhood, probing, probing, suggesting. He encouraged her to fantasize about how life might have been if she had made other choices. What might you have been? Who might you have been? What might you have done? What is your dream now? Is there any reason you couldn't become whatever you wanted even now?

He looked more into her past, her upbringing, and wondered aloud if she had ever felt, way below the surface, that she was constrained by her rigid, formalistic rearing.

"Were your parents all that saintly? Well-intentioned, sure, but was it the best for you?

"Did they encourage you to realize your own potential, or did they fit you into a life role?

"Did you have the freedom to sample and evaluate other views, or was your education planned and programmed?"

Over and over these "possible areas of conflict" were explored, all leading to her feelings about herself, her self-image, self-esteem, self-worth.

She began to agree with Dr. Finch that the sessions were becoming more productive as time passed. Edith felt she was in fact plumbing a deep well of resentment that had been building in her subconscious for years. It had been unknown and repressed. When she gave vent to these feelings and thoughts she had to admit that her parents had deprived her of the kind of love that would have given her freedom to follow her yearnings. They had been demeaning and negative toward her potential.

She reassessed her education in light of its doctrinaire approach and the resultant deprivation she suffered. In reality, she wasn't well-educated at all; she was narrow in her thinking and out of touch with the real world.

She wondered what life would have been like if she had not married the first man she met on campus. Her marriage had been a long-term commitment to service and she wondered if Bruce had any idea what she dreamed about or longed for. How could he? She hadn't allowed herself to let it surface, so even she hadn't been aware of it.

----------------------◆----------------------

"To be truly happy and fulfilled, you must fill your own love tank."

At church she was not a servant but a doormat, the first sucker everybody came to when they needed something done.

All the while Dr. Finch gently told her that these feelings had been there, below the surface, for years. "You repressed them behind a powerful facade of conformity. You'll remember that though I guided your thinking, I did not suggest these conclusions. You discovered them on your own. These are your own insights."

Edith became angry when new labels began coming to mind. She had come face-to-face with the fact that she was a pawn, a victim, used and abused by everyone in her orbit for as long as she could remember. No wonder she was devoid of self-esteem or feeling of significance.

She would never forget the day that Dr. Finch pulled his chair close to hers and spoke softly. "The most important human need is personal significance, a conviction of personal value. Without that bedrock you will never be able to really love others or even love God. How can you love anyone if you don't love yourself? Even the Bible says we're supposed to love others as we love ourselves. If you love others in the paltry way you love yourself, what kind of a love are you offering?

"To be truly happy and fulfilled, you must fill your own love tank. From what you have told me, your tank gauge is on empty. You must fill it to replace the love you thought was there from your parents and your own family."

He recommended that she begin a quest to repair her self-esteem. They would work together on her becoming more expressive and assertive. She might not get any respect if she didn't demand it. She was to set aside time for herself. Decide upon a career path and train for it, venture out on it.

Edith was to visualize herself as successful, respected, and authoritative. That technique would get her back on track if she became overcome by anxiety or fear in this deprogramming mode.

She went at her new life with gusto. Edith cut back on her church duties so she could study to get her real estate license. She began working full time, doing less at home and demanding that everyone pitch in. At first the family was proud of her and agreed this was a fair approach. But when she made one big sale and spent her commission on a new wardrobe, Edith began spending a lot of time on her looks.

Bruce had a difficult time adjusting to his new wife, but she passed that off as his having to come to grips with losing a slave. They were equals now, and he would have to take his share of the load. The kids complained that she was much more high strung and demanding than ever. To Edith this meant that she was getting some respect.

Bruce wondered what had happened to the plan of helping Jeff get back on track in school. Ironically, that problem had cleared itself up. Jeff finally admitted that he had suffered his first disappointment in love and had acted out his frustration with a little antisocial behavior. When he got over it and he and the girl were able to stay friends, the crisis passed. He had even decided on going to college and was investigating which one. Edith took credit for that, feeling that she had forced him to make a choice. But he had already resolved to do that.

Everything was working for Edith except her self-esteem. She was doing all those things she had been led to believe would make her the woman she was meant to be. But her house was not neat. Her family was not happy. She was less active in church. She was always uptight. She was not eating right. She was not happy, and she was blaming herself. That didn't sound like healthy self-esteem to Edith.

She began losing sleep, which affected her health, her job performance, and her looks. *Why am I not feeling the way Dr. Finch predicted I would? I'd rather be back in my old roles.*

Edith was soon depressed, suffering from constant headaches, and had no appetite. As the junior member of the sales office in her real estate company, she was the first to be laid off when the market went soft. She was devastated. Her boss told her she could still work on straight commission, but nothing was happening. The career that was supposed to have given back her dignity had betrayed her.

At home she was miserable. She hated herself, just the opposite of what was supposed to have happened. She took it out on Bruce and the boys, and she felt as if she were spiraling out of control. She didn't know who she was or what she wanted, but it certainly wasn't this. Dr. Finch urged her to not let her love tank drain out just because of some unfortunate incidents. He prescribed two tranquilizers and an antidepressant.

The day Edith found herself unable to get out of bed Bruce decided to take matters into his own hands. He called their family doctor, a longtime Christian friend. He made room for her that very day, not knowing what her symptoms were. Edith found herself strangely warmed by Bruce's take-charge attitude and was almost weepy with gratitude when he helped her get up and get dressed. He even fixed breakfast for her, but she just picked at it. By the time she got to the doctor she was nearly faint with a headache, and she was depressed.

"Just out of sorts and in need of a thorough checkup," was what Bruce had told their doctor, so the poor man had no idea what to expect. When he found Edith waiting in an examining room he picked up her chart and noted that he hadn't seen her in more than a year. He reached for his stethoscope and stopped in mid-gesture. Who was this pale, wan, drawn, under-weight, bags-under-the-eyes, empty woman who sat there?

"Edith," he said, "I don't want to be rude, but I hardly recognized you."

"It's been too long, I know," she said sheepishly.

The doctor, twenty years her senior, put his hands on her shoulders and waited for her eyes to meet his. "Edith," he said, "I hesitate to be so direct, but what's wrong, dear?"

She collapsed, sobbing. "I'm hopeless, depressed, all messed up!" she wailed. "Nothing in my life is turning out the way it was supposed to."

"You were one of the most vibrant Christian women I knew," he said. "What's going on?"

She told him the brief history of her therapy. He felt it best to take the direct approach. "Edith, listen to me. You're courting disaster. You must stop seeing your therapist and get off these medications. The whole course of therapy you've described is going to ruin you. It nearly already has."

From the end of her dark tunnel of depression Edith realized that she was hearing common sense and truth for the first time in a long time. The doctor confided later to Bruce: "That therapist may have claimed to be a Christian, but he was leading her into the arms of Satan, not the arms of Jesus. I'm convinced that if we hadn't been able to intervene, she'd have wound up committed, divorced, or even suicidal."

Bruce was angry. "I'd like to sue that Finch and get his license."

"The problem," his physician said, "is that he was very likely acting totally within the accepted methods of his profession. You have no idea how many people are being devastated by the very field that promises them hope."

The doctor prescribed drastic action. He urged Edith to return to the Bible study she'd had "no time for" for months. He recommended that she get involved again in volunteering at church. "Turn your focus outward, the way it always was. That is what is really fulfilling, serving others. There's nothing wrong with that. Jesus was no doormat, yet He served all of mankind, to the point of death."

"I feel like a sinner," Edith admitted.

"You were led into the sin of self-absorption. The Bible clearly says that to save our lives we have to lose them. You were in rebellion against what you knew was right for your life and spirit."

Edith still testifies about the release and relief that came that day when she got alone on her knees and thanked God for rescuing her. She asked His forgiveness for having worshipped at the altar of self.

It took many months, but Edith returned to serving God and others and says she feels even better now because she has a new lease on life. "I didn't know what a wonderful life I had until I gave it up to pursue a dream that was actually a nightmare."

9

Lovers of Self

◆———————◆

MANY EVANGELICAL LEADERS and some seminaries
have fought the battle over the inerrancy of
the Scriptures, and they have fought it well. However,
victory seems strangely empty as apostasy sweeps the
church. Inerrancy seems only to be of academic interest
as we ignore the Word as a doctrinal base for our teaching. Scripture may be inerrant, but it seems the church
does not intend to shape its thinking by it. Certainly this
refusal to do so is nowhere more evident than in the
acceptance of the thesis that man's most basic need is
for a sense of personal worth, a better self-image, and
higher self-esteem.

As Edith learned the hard way (see previous chapter), this idea is not only *foreign* to Scripture, but it is
also the very antithesis of biblical teaching. Yet only a
few lonely voices have challenged the self-esteem gospel, and those few have been labeled angry, divisive,

negative, "trash writers," and even as "carrying too much political baggage."

The message that God sent Jesus to die in order to fill our empty love tanks and thus make us feel better about ourselves is found nowhere in the Bible; yet our bookstores bulge with this lie. That inerrant Word God gave us tells us plainly that our need is for peace with a just and holy Creator.

God drove man out of the Garden of Eden, banishing him from the tree of life, even placing cherubim and a flaming sword to guard the entrance (Genesis 3:23,24). Wouldn't you assume that the gravity of this event would produce in man a genuine *lowering* of his self-esteem, a desire to obey his Creator, and a cry to God for mercy?

The building of the Tower of Babel is only one of the many records of man attempting to raise his self-esteem. Throughout all of history, most of mankind has failed to accept that making peace with an omnipotent Creator is necessary at all; much less have they recognized that to be their most basic ultimate need.

◆

> *Self-esteem is at*
> *the heart of our rebellion*
> *and is therefore certainly not*
> *a solution to our problems.*

The modern version of this refusal to accept our position before our Creator and Judge is the church's fascination with and acceptance of Erich Fromm's hierarchy of human needs. Fromm taught that man must learn to love himself before he can love anyone else; more accurately stated, this is the church's interpretation of Fromm's theory.

Since the author of Scripture is man's Creator, He obviously knows us better than we know ourselves. His Word makes it abundantly clear that since Eve ate the apple, not one of us has experienced any real problem loving self. The psychologists are not wrong in observing that man seeks security and significance. The church is wrong in failing to point this out as a mark of our fallen nature. This search is hardly characteristic of what Paul describes as "the new man in Christ."

That desire for "significance" is surely a large part of the reason Eve believed Satan when she was told "... when you eat of it your eyes will be opened, and you will be like God knowing good from evil" (Genesis 3:5). Since that time, all of mankind has exhibited that same difficulty in accepting his position as a creature before his Creator. When security and significance is seen as an acceptable goal in the church, we see Jesus as simply one more technique in our attempt to bypass that flaming sword blocking our entrance to life. Self-esteem is at the heart of our rebellion and is therefore certainly not a solution to our problems.

God has never permitted the elevation of self, and all of Scripture views it as rebellion.

> This is what the Sovereign Lord says: "In the pride of your heart you say, 'I am a god.' But you are a man and not a god, though you think you are as wise as a god. Your heart has grown proud. You were in Eden, the garden of God; wickedness was found in you. So I drove you in disgrace

from the mount of God, and I expelled you. Your heart became proud on account of your beauty, and you corrupted your wisdom because of your splendor" (from Ezekiel 28).

Having been made in the image of God, mankind has a certain beauty and splendor. "God saw all that he had made, and it was very good" (Genesis 1:31). However, it was for God's service and for God's glory that we were given any beauty and splendor. "You are worthy, our Lord and God, to receive glory and honor and power, for you created all things, and by your will they were created and have their being" (Revelation 4:11). "All things were created by him and for him" (Colossians 1:16).

The miserable church of the twentieth century tries hard to manufacture good feelings in its people. We are determined to avoid talk of sin and rebellion as the source of our bad feelings. After all, that might produce low self-esteem, which is viewed by modern man as the worst possible condition. The church is failing to remind people that it is only when we take our rightful place before our Creator that we find any real pleasure in life. Our pulpits, classes, books, and radio broadcasts tell us to assert ourselves, to repeat positive confessions every morning, to forgive ourselves, to remind ourselves aloud who we are in Christ, and to rebuke Satan because we are seated in the heavenlies, with all of Christ's power and authority! The solution is a ritual, and there seems no end to the self-centered games designed to make us feel better about ourselves.

The Bible teaches that a sentence of death has been imposed on us by our Creator. It says we are pardoned only when we accept by faith the atonement He provided for us by dying on the cross. We then become "servants of righteousness" by "wholeheartedly obeying that form of doctrine to which we were entrusted" (Romans 6:17). That form of doctrine teaches that we are to die to self daily, lose our lives daily, and carry our crosses daily.

The Messiah who paid such a costly price for us is never presented in Scripture as coming to make us feel better about ourselves. Jesus said, ". . . I came into the world, to testify to the truth . . ." (John 18:37). Yet when someone suggests to the modern church that truth is missing, the response is often like that of Pilate's: "What is truth? . . ." (John 18:38). As Jesus told Nicodemus in John 3:19, "This is the verdict: light has come into the world, but men loved darkness instead of light because their deeds were evil." Truth has been given us, the truth that will set us free (John 8:32), but we prefer Freud in the name of "science."

We don't want to hear that our deeds are evil. The words are no more pleasant to our ears than they were to Nicodemus, who was well aware of the prestige he stood to lose if he believed what Jesus was saying. The refusal to acknowledge this truth concerning the heart of man is why most of the people said 2000 years ago, "If he didn't come to give me comfort and relief [bread and power] right now, crucify him!" Many in today's church would say the same.

Fromm, of course, did not base his hierarchy of human needs on the Bible, and in that he was far more honest than is the church. In spite of overwhelming numbers of Bible passages to the contrary, the church has joined society in blaming low self-image for academic difficulties, bad behavior in children, divorce, crime, poverty, and even illness. Instead of speaking God's truth to a society lost in this delusion, the church misses that tremendous opportunity and fills people with the same delusion.

We no longer hear the Golden Rule: "In everything, do to others what you would have them do to you, for this sums up the Law and the Prophets." The obvious interpretation of this passage is that Jesus—our Creator—knew that we treat ourselves well, think highly of ourselves, and want only the best for ourselves. It is a cultic twisting of Scripture to suggest that the human being has difficulty loving himself and for this reason has problems obeying the Golden Rule (Matthew 7:12).

The Ten Commandments are directed toward our need to love God and others. Considering the entirety of God's Word, it would be not only incongruous but also absurd for God to have descended in fire onto Mt. Sinai, making the mountain tremble (Exodus 19:18), in order to command us to love ourselves.

Only a few of the verses speaking directly to this issue:

Matthew 19:30: "But many who are first will be last, and many who are last will be first."

Matthew 18:4: "Therefore, whoever humbles himself like this child is the greatest in the kingdom of heaven."

Luke 14:26: "If anyone comes to me and does not hate...his own life—he cannot be my disciple."

Luke 9:24: "Whoever wants to save his life will lose it, but whoever loses his life for me will find it."

Luke 18:14: "...For everyone who exalts himself will be humbled, and he who humbles himself will be exalted."

John 12:25: "The man who loves his life will lose it, while the man who hates his life in this world will keep it for eternal life."

James 4:10: "Humble yourself before the Lord, and he will lift you up."

1 Peter 5:5: "... Clothe yourselves with humility toward one another, because, 'God opposes the proud but gives grace to the humble.' Humble yourselves, therefore, under God's mighty hand...."

Where do we find anything in Scripture even remotely resembling the self-esteem gospel? Paul plainly tells us in Philippians 2 that our attitude is to be like that of Jesus, "who, being in very nature God, did not consider equality with God something to be grasped, but made himself nothing, taking the very nature of a servant" (verses 6-7).

God's real leaders will never be produced from the leadership training courses so plentiful today. God does not choose His leaders based on their high self-image. Moses is described in Numbers 12:3 as "the meekest man on earth." When God called Moses to leadership in Exodus 3 and 4, Moses did not say, "I wondered when you would finally get around to recognizing my gifts. After all, I am one of the Chosen People; remember what a special baby I was, raised in Pharaoh's palace, recipient of the best of Egypt's education! If only you hadn't waited so long, I had all the right connections. Now that fellow Hebrew has humiliated me by asking, 'Who made you ruler and judge over us?' I've had to battle demons of self-doubt every day since then. I was beginning to wonder when all those positive confessions I've made were ever going to pay off!"

No, the Scriptures do not record Moses fleeing to Midian to work on his self-image. Instead, God calls

Moses only after years of humbling on that backside of the desert. When He does call, Moses replies, "Who am I that I should go to Pharaoh and bring the Israelites out of Egypt? I have never been eloquent; I am slow of speech and tongue." The Bible tells us that Moses hid his face because he was afraid to look on God.

Note that God did not say, "Now Moses, you have an unrealistically low opinion of yourself. We can't work together until you build your self-image. Don't you know you're really wonderful and the Trinity would be at such a loss if we didn't come to get you here in Midian. After all, you're destined for the throne."

No, God simply said, "I will be with you" (Exodus 3:12).

When God called Gideon (Judges 6), we have no picture of a brazen, bold warrior who had been self-actualized via self-esteem therapy. Instead we are told that Gideon was threshing his wheat in a winepress to remain hidden from the Midianites. God's great leader-to-be was hiding! His response to God's call to lead Israel was not: "Well, after all, I was made in God's image and born into one of the tribes of God's chosen people. That tells me right there that I'm of great worth. I'm ready to claim my victory—in Your name, of course."

No, Judges 6:15 records Gideon: "How can I save Israel? My clan is the weakest . . . and I am the least in my family." God did not say He couldn't use a man with such a low opinion of himself. Instead, God said, "I will be with you."

When Isaiah saw the Lord (Isaiah 6), he did not say, "I wondered when I would get this vision, since I have such godly concern for this nation."

No, Isaiah cried, "Woe to me! I am ruined! For I am a man of unclean lips and I live among a people of unclean lips, and my eyes have seen the King, the Lord Almighty."

God did not respond, "That's a negative world view, Isaiah. I'll teach you to visualize away those awful feelings the next time they come upon you." Instead, God said, "Your sin is atoned for."

When God called Jeremiah to be his prophet to Judah, Jeremiah did not answer, "Well, I *am* a son of Hilkiah, one of the priests of Anathoth. I'm qualified, and I don't have as many demons in my ancestral line as so many of the people have now."

No, Jeremiah responded, "I do not know how to speak, Sovereign Lord. I am only a child."

And God simply said, "I am with you and will rescue you."

To the end of his days, Jeremiah maintained the biblical world view that he recorded in Lamentations 3:22: "Because of the Lord's great love we are not consumed, for his compassions never fail." This stands in contrast to today's theology that God does not eliminate His rebellious people because they are so special.

Jeremiah knew that we live and breathe due only to God's great love and mercy.

Samson served God only after being reduced to a blind prisoner.

King David sat before the Lord and said, "Who am I . . . and what is my family, that you have brought me this far?" (from 2 Samuel 7:18, authors' paraphrase).

When Solomon became king, he did not see his success depending on a sense of self-worth. Instead, he answered God, "I'm only a child and do not know how to carry out my duties, so give your servant a discerning heart to govern your people and to distinguish right from wrong. For who is able to govern?"

If ever there was a man in whom God might approve self-esteem, it should have been Job. Job is described as "blameless and upright, fearing God and shunning evil." However, God did not respond to Job's suffering by leading a workshop to help him understand what a fine man he actually was and to make him realize that he was an innocent victim of that mean old devil.

It should be clear to any reader of the book of Job that Satan's attacks were not punishment for sin. Equally clear is that the answer to Job's troubles did not lie in mobilizing prayer warriors to fight the invisible enemy who appeared to be foiling God's plan for this upright man. God did not instruct Job, his family, or his friends in techniques for wrestling with dark angels.

Instead, then the Lord answered Job out of the storm. He said: "Who is this who darkens my counsel with words without knowledge? ... Where were you when I laid the earth's foundation? Tell me if you understand. Who marked off its dimensions? Surely you know!..." (Job 38:1-5). God continued in this vein, leaving no doubt that our knowledge of Him is not only limited, but minuscule. Oh, that today's church would say with Job, "Surely, I spoke of things I did not understand, things too wonderful for me to know. My ears had heard of you but now my eyes have seen you. Therefore, I despise myself and repent in dust and ashes."

Job was not one who needed long-term therapy for low self-image. Rather, God says to Job's friends (the men who claimed to understand the unseen struggle in the heavens), "You have not spoken of me what is right as my servant Job has. Go to my servant Job and sacrifice a burnt offering for yourselves. My servant Job will pray for you and I will accept his prayer and not deal with you according to your folly."

The sovereign Lord does not take lightly our attempts to identify and command the demons. He does not see as a mere aberration our efforts to avoid repentance while we build up the self. God would surely say to us, "I am angry with you because you have not spoken of me what is right as my servant Job has."

Our prayer is that today's church would cease to obscure God's counsel without knowledge (Job 42:3).

The Bible is so incredibly consistent in the bringing down of the proud and the lifting up of the humble that one has to wonder what has bewitched the church. How can it claim Scripture as its authority and blend the psychological gospel of self-esteem into its theology? Surely this evidences an increasing absence of a fear of God.

A.J. Conyers, chairman of the Department of Religion and Philosophy at Charleston Southern University, describes this in his book *The Eclipse of Heaven*. When Hurricane Hugo hit the city of Charleston, Conyers notes among the population an absence of awareness of the power of God over creation and of the frailty of the human condition. He describes the situation: "Even in the extremities of natural disaster, we no longer ask how this illuminates the mystery 'over us,' but instead attend to the enigma 'within us.'" He tells how the local radio stations brought on psychologists and psychiatrists to supposedly help people through their stages of grief. Sadly, the response of the church to this kind of self-centered emptiness in society is simply to bring out their own psychologists and psychiatrists, mix in a few Jesus-words, and give messages no less empty and destructive.

A few of the many verses on the fear of God:

Psalm 19:9: "The fear of the LORD is pure, enduring forever..."

Psalm 103:17: "From everlasting to everlasting, the Lord's love is with those who fear him."

Proverbs 1:7: "The fear of the LORD is the beginning of knowledge, but fools despise wisdom and discipline."

Proverbs 15:33: "The fear of the LORD teaches a man wisdom, and humility comes before honor."

Proverbs 16:5: "The LORD detests all the proud of heart. Be sure of this: They will not go unpunished."

Proverbs 19:23: "The fear of the LORD leads to life..."

Proverbs 22:4: "Humility and the fear of the LORD bring wealth and honor and life."

Malachi 3:2,16,17: "Who can endure the day of his coming? Who can stand when he appears?...Then those who feared the Lord talked with each other, and the LORD listened and heard. A scroll of remembrance was written in his presence concerning those who feared the LORD and honored his name. 'They will be mine,' says the LORD Almighty, 'in the day when I make up my treasured possession. I will spare them, just as in compassion a man spares his son who serves him.'"

Luke 1:50: "His mercy extends to those who fear him..."

Fear is viewed in the church today much as it is in the world: as a sign of pathology needing psychiatric intervention. Is this why we see no George Whitefield or John Bunyan in the modern church? These men experienced such fear at their conversions that today we would lock them away.

Arnold Dallimore, in *George Whitefield* (Banner Of Truth)—his biography of the man Martyn Lloyd-Jones called "the greatest preacher England ever produced"—describes Whitefield as "subject to strange and terrible emotions." In Whitefield's own words: "A horrible fearfulness and dread was permitted to overwhelm my soul, weight upon my breast attended with inward darkness. All power of meditating or even thinking was taken from me. I could fancy myself to be like nothing so much as a man locked up in iron armor." His scholastic work at Oxford suffered from this fearful preoccupation of his mind, and he describes his tutor as "enquiring whether any misfortune has befallen me. I burst into tears and assured him it was not out of contempt for authority but that I could not act otherwise. Then at length, he said he believed I could not and when he left me, told a friend as he very well might, that he took me to be really mad."[1]

Dallimore describes Whitefield's conversion: "When he had come to an end of all human resources, when there was nothing else he could do to seek salvation, God revealed Himself in grace, and granted him that which he had found could never be earned. In a sense of utter desperation, in rejection of all self-trust, he cast his soul on the mercy of God through Jesus Christ, and a ray of faith, granted him from above, assured him he would not be cast out."

Whitefield himself described it: "God was pleased to remove the heavy load, to enable me to lay hold of His dear Son by a living faith. O! With what joy—joy unspeakable—even joy that was full of and big with glory was my soul filled when the weight of sin went off, and an abiding sense of the pardoning love of God and a full assurance of faith broke in upon my disconsolate soul!"

John Newton, the converted slave trader who wrote "Amazing Grace," had a scriptural view of fear:

> 'Twas grace that taught my heart to fear
> And grace those fears relieved.
> How wondrous did that grace appear,
> The hour I first believed.

John Bunyan also understood the fear of God and seems also to have understood the attempt to avoid that fear. He described this when he wrote of the theology of the man he called Ignorance:

> Fear tends much to men's good and to make them right at their beginning to go on pilgrimage. True or right fear is discovered by three things:
>
> 1. By its rise; it is caused by saving conviction for sin.
> 2. It driveth the soul to lay fast hold of Christ for salvation.
> 3. It begetteth and continueth in the soul a great reverence of God, His Word, and ways.
>
> The ignorant know not that such convictions as tend to put them in fear are for their good, and therefore, they seek to stifle them.

1. They think these fears are wrought by the devil (though indeed they are wrought of God) and thinking so, they resist them.

◆

Self-esteem and the fear of God cannot be integrated, and a glance at the church of the '90s leaves no doubt as to which of those has been eliminated.

---

2. They think these fears tend to the spoiling of their faith; when alas for them, they have none at all, and therefore they harden their hearts against them.

3. They presume they ought not to fear and therefore, in despite of them, wax presumptuously confident.

4. They see that those fears tend to take away from them their pitiful old self-holiness and therefore, they resist them with all their might.[2]

Self-esteem and the fear of God cannot be integrated, and a glance at the church of the '90s leaves no doubt as to which of those has been eliminated. It is commonly accepted that people who seek the high positions, rude and arrogant people, as well as disobedient children all suffer from low self-esteem and are not getting enough love and attention. Parents agonize over how to give their rebellious child more love, more praise, more of anything that will make him feel good about himself. Discipleship groups have become sensitivity training therapy sessions on how to make everyone feel better about themselves.

We are told to avoid presenting the gospel until we have "corrected the father image," gained a person's trust, and given him significance. Our "gospel" becomes a story of how Jesus offers security and personal worth. (It is never quite clear how this Jesus does a better job of this than does money, power, or yoga.) Who needs a Savior when we can become peaceful and "corrected" without any God coming to bleed?

How silly it all sounds! These ideas are utterly foreign to Scripture, and this should greatly alarm the church.

> Do not be deceived: God cannot be mocked....The one who sows to please his sinful nature, from that nature will reap destruction (Galatians 6:7-8).

> These people honor me with their lips, but their hearts are far from me. They worship in vain; their teachings are but rules taught by men. You have let go of the commands of God and are holding on to the traditions of men (Mark 7:6-8).

> Woe to you...you hypocrites! You travel over land and sea to win a single convert, and when he becomes one, you make him twice as much a son of hell as you are (Matthew 23:15).

The gentle Jesus taught doctrinal truth. He never hinted that the arrogant false shepherds of Israel had self-esteem problems that explained their desire to stand in the synagogues and on the street corners to be seen by men. In Luke 12, Jesus does not describe as insecure the rich man who was living for today. Rather, He labels him a fool who will get what he has coming to him that very night when his life is demanded of him.

Moses made sure Israel understood that it was not because of their righteousness or self-worth that God would give them the land. He calls them a stiff-necked people and reminds them that God is giving them the land to accomplish what He promised to Abraham (Deuteronomy 9:4-6).

Would anyone today witness as did Stephen (Acts 7:51): "You stiff-necked people, with uncircumcised hearts and ears!...You always resist the Holy Spirit! ...You have betrayed and murdered him—you who have received the law that was put into effect through angels but have not obeyed it."

Stephen's major concern was obviously not their feelings of self-worth or sense of significance. On the other hand, our human-potential message doesn't get us stoned to death. Stephen's message was not popular. Is this one of the reasons the psychological gospel is so attractive to the church?

"I am not ashamed of the gospel, because it is the power of God for the salvation of everyone who believes" (Romans 1:16). We seem ashamed of that gospel Paul delivered so faithfully. Most of us are not joining Episcopal Bishop John Spong in labeling the apostle Paul a homosexual. Yet our psychologized doctrine clearly assumes Paul to have been a man in need of recovery treatment. He called himself "chief among sinners" and "wretched man that I am." He worked day and night without concern for burnout, a true "workaholic" (1 Thessalonians 1). He admits to conflicts on the outside, fears within (1 Corinthians 7:5), pressure beyond his ability to endure, despairing even of life itself (2 Corinthians 8), seeing messengers from Satan as sent by God to keep him from being conceited (2 Corinthians 12:7). He even said his power was made perfect in weakness, and for that reason he delighted in weakness, insults, hardships, and persecution (2 Corinthians 1:12). How different church history would be if therapists had been available to help this poor man learn to love himself and thus move toward mental health!

What does the record of Scripture show as the reward for those who believed, obeyed, and followed the true gospel?

Paul's last word to us from a cold prison in Rome:

"Demas, because he loved this world, has deserted me. Bring the cloak that I left at Troas and my scrolls. Alexander the metalworker did me a great deal of harm. No one came to my support, everyone deserted me" (from 2 Timothy 4).

Peter, who served God so faithfully after being humbled, was told by Jesus:

> "I tell you the truth, when you were younger [and full of self-esteem] you dressed yourself and went where you wanted; but when you are old [and are my humble servant] you will stretch out your hands, and someone else will dress you and lead you where you do not want to go." Jesus said this to indicate the kind of death by which Peter would glorify God

[crucified upside down under Nero] (John 21:18-19).

John the Baptist was said of Jesus to be the greatest of those born of women (Matthew 11:11). He was also the one who humbled himself, saying he was not fit to carry Jesus' sandals (Matthew 3:11). This servant of God died by execution in prison.

Does the church follow the false gospel of psychology because of its promise of earthly reward here and now?

Paul knew this to be our nature and wrote:

> The message of the cross is foolishness to those who are perishing, but to us who are being saved, it is the power of God.... Where is the wise man? Where is the scholar? Where is the philosopher of this age? Has not God made foolish the wisdom of the world? (1 Corinthians 1:18,20).

Christian magazines carry ads offering books on healing memories, satisfying your love hunger, getting more for yourself, Christian therapy, user-friendly churches, outrageous joy, engaging the evening, breaking through to spiritual maturity, and your personal plan for finding significance.

The church blindly goes in this direction, while even the secular world recognizes it as wrong for those who claim to believe God. *Time* magazine, April 5, 1993, ends its article entitled "The Church Search": "Many of those who have rediscovered churchgoing may ultimately be shortchanged, however, if the focus of their faith seems subtly to shift from the glorification of God to the gratification of man."

In our opinion, the shift is no longer subtle.

Can we ignore Paul's admonition to the Galatian church? Today he would surely say it this way: "You foolish church leaders! Who has bewitched you? Before your very eyes, Christ is clearly portrayed in Scripture as crucified and the Christian life as one of carrying a cross and losing your life. I am astonished that you are so quickly deserting the One who called you by the grace of Christ and are turning to a different gospel which is really no good news at all. I remind you, if an M.D. or a Ph.D. or a 'visualized Jesus' preaches to you a gospel other than the one we preached, let him be eternally condemned—no matter what his qualifications in the eyes of the world. If I were still trying to please men, I would not be a servant of Christ. The gospel I preached is not something men made up. I did not receive it from any man, nor was I taught it . . . rather, I received it from Christ by revelation. You are becoming again children of the slave woman—burdened again by a yoke of slavery" (Galatians 1,3).

A false gospel always brings bondage. Our techniques never end; our therapy sessions go on until either our bodies can no longer climb the stairs to the counselor's office or our insurance coverage runs out. We can never claim enough promises or find the right words to achieve the level of warfare-praying we really need (Matthew 6:7,8). Eventually we collapse, bleeding and exhausted.

The question remains: Will we see the truth as did Martin Luther after all his wrong directions? Or will we curse God, having been told by our therapist that letting out our anger will keep us from depression? (After all, "God's a big boy; He can take it.")

Those accepting the true gospel believe with Peter that we have an inheritance kept in heaven (1 Peter 1:4), and with Paul that the Lord will bring us safely to his heavenly kingdom (2 Timothy 4:18), and with Jesus that we should rejoice and be glad in the hard times, because great is our reward in heaven (Matthew 5:22).

They will come to agree with C.T. Studd, that faithful Englishman who left Cambridge University to spend his life as a missionary in Africa: "If Christ be God, and He died for me, let nothing I might ever do be called a sacrifice."

10

Roy's Forever Co-Dependent Recovery

◆————◆

D R. ROY SNYDER HAD BEEN an up-and-comer. He sailed through medical school with top grades, despite being known for his prodigious drinking and love of a good time. He shone as an intern and soon moved on to seemingly realize the dream he had talked so much about in med school. He had always said he wanted to be "successful, well-known, and rich. And why not?"

Roy was soon known as one of the top young internists in his suburb. His practice moved from one impressive suite of offices to another every few years. He and his wife bought a mansion in the toniest area, wore designer clothes, each had an obscenely expensive luxury car, and they belonged to all the right clubs and associations.

His material success came much earlier in his career than it had for his peers. Any jealousy was manifest in comments about his workaholism. Roy was always on call. He could be summoned off the golf course any time, rarely took vacations, and had the most extensive office and hospital hours of anyone in the county.

His friends could only shake their heads. He was still the life of any party, and everyone knew he had fulfilled his dream by simply raking in the profits from his high tolerance for work. Every patient, every case spelled cash for Roy, but people feared he would work himself to death before he was 40.

Roy was on call for the emergency room at Hillside Hospital, and once, when a case proved to be a false alarm, he spent nearly half an hour bouncing ideas off the office staff. "What would make you leave your family doctor, your general practitioner, and come see a new doctor?" he would ask.

◆

What people couldn't know, of course, was that behind closed doors in that beautiful home was trouble.

The people in the E.R. shrugged.

"What if a doctor with an office in a swankier part of town offered a good deal, maybe even something free? The thought of having the rich people's doctor evaluating your X-rays would be appealing, wouldn't it? How about a free blood test, or chest X-ray, or even a physical?"

"Buy one, get one free," one of the nurses teased.

"Not a bad idea," Dr. Roy said. "Bring a friend for another penny!" Everyone roared. But Roy had not been kidding. It wasn't long before his high-profile practice had a jammed parking lot and people standing in line to sign up for routine checkups. He worked feverishly to convert them into paying customers.

It wasn't that he was a bad guy. He certainly didn't tell anyone they needed medical work when they didn't. But he knew full well that a certain percentage of any population benefits from some kind of internal medicine workup. Even if all the patient needed was a laxative, Roy worked hard on his bedside manner and won himself a long-term patient. When something did go seriously wrong, he would be back.

What people couldn't know, of course, was that behind closed doors in that beautiful home was trouble. Roy's wife and his kids were complaining that he wasn't home enough. "You don't complain about all the stuff I buy you!" Roy would snap back.

The truth was he was living beyond even his already substantial income. The cars, the mortgage, and the rent on his suite of offices alone cost nearly half his monthly income. The extras, the parties, the clothes, the gifts, the dinners, the memberships, had him buried.

Roy felt the pressure most intensely when his CPA informed him that his income was much less than his obligations. He had to keep working and working just to stay afloat. Everything he did dug a deeper hole, so there could be no breaks, no vacations. He and his wife agreed they would have to cut back on discretionary spending, but only where it showed. For instance, they would not be trading up to that new Lexus. She would get another year out of the BMW. Both would mix and match their wardrobes more and take a hiatus from buying clothes for a while. In the spring they might each buy something that made it appear they had started over for the season.

Only Roy's wife, Julie, knew the truth about his drinking. It was no longer just a nightcap or a few shots at a party. It was no longer only a six-pack on Sunday. Roy seemed to be drinking constantly. When his friends would "have one" before lunch, he would have two, then one during the meal, and another afterward. He had built a tolerance to hard liquor that allowed him—at least in his own mind—to function without it showing.

He knew enough to use cologne and breath fresheners so no patient or colleague would smell the booze on him during the day. He even talked to Julie about knowing he had "to get this under control. When we get out from under these bills, I'll be able to get a handle on it. Meanwhile, it's the only way I know to relax."

She tried arguing with him on it and even tried to talk him out of "just one more" at home, but she quickly learned that was counterproductive. He became surly when he was denied his alcohol, and if she needed or wanted anything from him, she did better to provide drinks than to prohibit them. When she would came home with a supply of his favorite whisky, he was nearly overcome with gratitude.

Julie was under the impression that she was doing the right thing by him finally, because he frequently came home in the evening saying he was allowed two or three drinks because he hadn't had one all day. Well, maybe that one after-lunch drink. She casually mentioned that to one of the colleagues he often ate with, and he confirmed it. "He's cutting back," the man said. "I know I'm impressed."

What Julie didn't know was that Roy had been substituting marijuana during the day. The smell was easier to camouflage, and he felt very relaxed and much more in control. When one of the women in the office asked if he could "scare" her boyfriend out of his cocaine habit, Roy tried. The young man said, "Doc, if you snorted one line of coke, you'd never want anything else as long as you lived."

Roy was intrigued, but he couldn't let on. Rather, he took it as a challenge. "I'll bet I could sample it and never do it again." He bet the boy the cost of the cocaine. And lost. They entered into an agreement whereby the young man provided the coke and Roy charged the kid's insurance company for the drug rehabilitation counseling. They did coke frequently and held the secret over each other's heads. Roy felt terrible when the young woman in the office frequently thanked him for the work he was doing with her boyfriend.

Drugs and alcohol are a time bomb, of course, and it wasn't long before Roy's work showed the effects. In January he was frantically working on a critically injured child when he began screaming for the lab work. He needed to know important details to know what to prescribe. The kid was in bad shape.

"I'm sorry, Doctor," the E.R. nurse said, "but I don't think anyone has taken blood yet. Did you ask us to get a workup done?"

"Of course, I did!" he said, swearing. "I'm flying blind here! Now get it done!"

The ebullient doctor had never shown such anger, and the nurse passed it off as pressure from the crisis.

But it wasn't the short temper that bothered her so—even though it was exposed before waiting patients. What really got to her was that she was certain the doctor had not asked anyone to take blood and have the lab evaluate it. In fact, she had nearly suggested it, but she had learned that most doctors appreciate helpful hints almost as much as they like second-guessing. She had once reminded a doctor of something, and he later wrote her up for being insubordinate.

Fortunately, the boy was quickly stabilized, "no thanks to the E.R. staff," Roy muttered, but later that same month he nearly lost a patient through negligence. A local convalescent home rushed in an elderly man who was delirious and feverish. "Just needs hydration," Dr. Snyder said. "Fix him up with the fluids and they can administer it at the home."

The E.R. nurse was stunned that he had not asked for a routine chest X-ray to rule out other causes. "He could have pneumonia," she said to a colleague, horrified to realize Roy had overheard.

"Oh, thank you, Nurse Know-It-All," he said. "Or should I call you Doctor?"

"No, I'm sorry, it's just that—"

"It's just that you want more insurance companies on my neck for overprescribing or overtesting. That's all I need."

"Sorry, Doctor. I'm sure you know best."

"I'm sure I do."

The next day the nurse got a call from the hospital administrator's secretary. "Just thought you'd want to know. A formal complaint is being filed against the E.R. for a misdiagnosis." She read off the name of the patient Roy had treated the day before.

"Yes," the nurse said, "Dr. Snyder treated him."

"Dr. Snyder is usually right on target."

"I know."

"Well, the patient is at another hospital this morning, battling pneumonia that could have been detected yesterday with a simple chest X-ray."

In February, the E.R. nurse felt she had to take matters into her own hands. When Roy prescribed clearly the wrong antibiotic for a young, pregnant woman, she challenged him. "Doctor, I'm sorry, but I wouldn't be doing my job if I didn't speak up."

Roy sighed. "We used to be friends. What's the deal with your constant second-guessing?"

"We are still friends, sir. But we've been told that the ingredients in the antibiotic you prescribed can have serious side effects and jeopardize the pregnancy."

"Just stay off my back!" Roy said.

The nurse phoned the infectious disease department and asked if that drug should ever be prescribed during a pregnancy. "Only if you want a wrongful death on your conscience," she was told.

She called the hospital pharmacy. "Fortunately we're out of that right now," they reported, "so the young woman was likely sent to her own drugstore."

The nurse quickly checked the records, then phoned the patient's pharmacy. "I'm glad you called," the pharmacist said. "Some jerk over there prescribed the wrong antibiotic for our customer. Side effects are one thing, but endangering a life is another."

The nurse caught Roy before he left the hospital. "We've got to talk," she said.

"I've got appointments waiting."

"Talk to me now or I file a grievance with the review board."

He glared at her. "You're cruising," he said.

"You're the one courting disaster," she said.

"All right, what?"

She led him back to her cubicle and told him of the antibiotic fiasco.

"You made those phone calls behind my back?"

"I saved your neck," she said. "You're my friend, but this was serious. This is going to get back to the administration here, just like that old man with pneumonia did."

"We can still cover that," Roy said, beginning to sweat. "You can remember that I did say something about getting an X-ray and that a nurse's aid or somebody, someone we can't remember, said it would be done or had been done or something."

"Roy, they've already let you off on that one with a note in your file. This is the one you've got to worry about."

"Well, we're friends. You've got to cover for me. Tell them I was the one who noticed the error on the prescription and that I told you to call pharmacy and the drugstore right away. You can do that, can't you?"

"If it was true I could," she said. "I might even be able to talk myself into that if I thought it was an honest mistake. But, Roy, you're not the doctor you used to be. You're dangerous."

Roy leaned forward, tears in his eyes. "What'll it take? You need some money?"

"Doctor!"

"C'mon, I can't afford to lose this gig. I've got expenses."

"It isn't this gig you should be worrying about, Roy. You lose your position here, it gets all over town. You could lose everything."

"I know! How can you do this to me?"

"Because I need you to start thinking about the patients! They're more important than your bills. What's gotten into you?"

"Okay, listen, you're right. I promise I'll get my head on straight and do better. Only this has got to stay between us, all right?"

She shook her head. "I really think it's too late, Roy."

"You would do this to me?"

"You've done this to yourself."

He set his jaw. "I'll be forced to turn the guns on you."

"Like what?"

"Don't think I can't come up with some stories on you, reasons you would want to tell lies about me."

She leaned back in her chair. "Oh, Roy," she said sadly.

"'Oh, Roy' is right," said a voice from the next cubicle, causing both doctor and nurse to jump. The E.R. secretary stood and peered down on them over the partition. "I heard all that, Dr. Snyder. You just buried yourself."

Roy ran out for a drink, snorted some coke, and raced home where he collapsed into bed. Julie made excuses for him all afternoon. His office had to cancel all his appointments, and of course the hospital administrator wanted to talk to him right away.

The hospital peer review committee met in emergency session the next afternoon, and Roy was required to be there. He showed up sober, glib, and looking his best. No one would look him in the eye as they asked him hard questions and heard his surprisingly lucid answers.

_____

He admitted his mistake on the pneumonia case, acted surprised to hear that the blood work snafu had reached them, and said he had a clear recollection of having asked for it. Secretly he worried whether his conversation with the E.R. nurse had been reported. When he was asked about that most serious incident, he explained that he recalled having made a serious error at the same time others recognized it. "I was just about to make those calls when I heard that they had already been made. Was I relieved! I'm not perfect, and I really blew that one. I'm just thankful we caught it in time and that my colleagues were there for me."

The committee thanked him and dismissed him. He took the same route home and to bed, thinking he had done well. Still he needed booze and dope to comfort him, and he slept as his wife played receptionist. The next morning he was visited at his office by Dr. William Metcalf, a colleague at the hospital.

He and Bill had been buddies since med school but had drifted apart during the last year, seeing each other only on social occasions due to Roy's workload. "Bill! Come in!"

"I'll get right to the point, Roy," Dr. Metcalf said. "Because I'm your friend, I've been asked to bring you the decision of the committee. It's binding, as you know."

"Unless I file suit," Roy said, suddenly rigid and panicky.

"You don't want to do that, Roy. We have come to the best possible conclusion in this case. Anything else would ruin you. You know with your lapses we could have concluded that you were misbehaving, sloppy, or in need of discipline or punishment. Rather, we see that you're a substance abuser and you need to be rehabilitated."

"Me? Are you kidding?"

"Roy, take it. If you don't go for rehab, we report you to the state licensing board and remove your hospital privileges. You get yourself straightened out and you're back on the job."

"In how long?"

"I guess that depends on what a model patient you are."

Roy wondered who would pay his bills in the meantime. "I'm no alcoholic, Bill. You know that."

"From just watching you at parties, Roy, I'd have to disagree. I'd say you've developed into a full-blown drunk, and you need help. Friend to friend, buddy, take this."

———————————————◆———————————————

> *In order to appear open and accessible to all, the staff made every effort to represent Jesus not in what they termed the "fixed and limited" version contained in the Bible.*

Roy knew he had no choice, but he went kicking and screaming to the Executive Renewal Program at the Willow Rest Christian Rehabilitation Treatment Center. He was defiant, angry, and defensive, coming up with excuse after excuse about why he had been railroaded by "former friends." Even his wife blamed the peer review committee and accused them of jealousy.

By the end of the first week, however, Roy had succumbed to the relentless pressure of the other patients and the therapy team. It was a major breakthrough when he stood before the group and tearfully admitted that he was a drunk and a substance abuser and that it was ruining his life.

His wife quickly joined him and admitted that she must have been co-dependent because she had bordered on enabling behavior. As part of a 12-step recovery program, based on the 12 steps in the Alcoholics Anonymous movement, Roy had leaped the first hurdle. He admitted he needed the help of a higher power, that he was beyond his own strength.

As the others in the group embraced him and encouraged him, he collapsed in tears and experienced an emotional release he had never known. Now it all made sense. He felt free to tell his story in comfort and safety. He opened himself to others with the same problems. They were further along the road to recovery, so he could visualize a future of complete freedom, with their help.

Being a Christian organization, Willow Rest saw as its mission the delivery of the tried-and-true 12-step recovery process to Christians. To them it was the best of both worlds. Jesus was the higher power. He would make the psychotherapy work. Only through Him could a patient feel good about himself and achieve self-actualization.

In order to appear open and accessible to all, the staff made every effort to represent Jesus not in what they termed the "fixed and limited" version contained in the Bible, but rather as an ideal image of the earthly father that addicts never had.

The subtle message from Willow Rest was that drunkenness was not a fruit of our sin nature, but rather a result of our rearing. The "Willow Rest Jesus" helped clients remember the trauma of their upbringing in order to go through a forgiveness ritual, visualizing that abuser who made them drink and use drugs. Willow Rest therapists viewed their clients as products of their environment with some predisposition to the disease of alcoholism programmed into their genes. Willow Rest told Roy and his wife that they could use Jesus' power to achieve self-love, self-acceptance, and self-authentication so as to eliminate the need for drink, drugs, and co-dependency. This would in turn transform their lives and reform their relationship.

Roy was swept along into never-ending "recovery methods" where hours were spent combing his childhood for reasons for his behavior. Graduates of the rehabilitation program accepted that they would need years of ongoing group therapy. Healing of inner hurts would take a lifetime.

Roy and his wife went from resisters to zealots. Drawing on the strength of his winsome personality, Roy became a star pupil. He and Julie raced through the 12 steps and became facilitators who would later become recovery group leaders. At every meeting, Roy stood and identified himself as an alcoholic.

Roy was caught up in Christianized recovery and continued to search his past for trauma and abuse. In chapter 3 we discussed the Pseudo-memory Pandemic. The False Memory Syndrome Foundation was formed by and for parents who claim to have been falsely accused by their children of horribly abusing them years before. These accusations stem from the "discovery" of memories during psychotherapy, with or without hypnosis. These parents are working to expose this damaging effect of psychotherapy, to warn others, to help each other, and to try to reach their bitterly estranged daughters and sons.

Their stories more recently are being told in the media. More and more accusing children are coming forward as "recanters," realizing their "therapy" was destructive to all. Successful lawsuits have been filed by parents and former patients themselves. The American Psychological Association has charged a task force to examine the issue and make recommendations. This news and the fact that you are reading this book are gratifying signs that one more psychobabble fad may be passing from the scene.

Expect the recovery industry to fight back. Expect clever and convincing tactics. Two recent seminars offer to help recovery advocates understand what they call "backlash."

In February of 1994 the Illinois Alcohol and Other Drug Abuse Professional Certification Association, Inc. held a workshop on "The False Memory Debate." Its brochure states, "The substance abuse and mental health treatment field is being challenged on almost a daily basis... In many cases therapists are being singled out as the problem, and in some cases are being sued by their patients."

The January issue of the *IAODAPCA News* (with a logo containing "steps to professionalism") contained an article by the guest speaker at the seminar, "a therapist in private practice ... specializing in working with adult children and co-dependents." The author decries the "backlash against the recovery movement" as populated by parents who "attempt to remove their responsibility for having abused their child and tr[y] to invalidate the child's experience of

194

having been abused." He laments that the adult child and/or co-dependent victim may be influenced by the claims of the "false memory advocates" to doubt their memories and even "blame themselves for it all over again...even though we are in recovery and know differently." He adds that "survivors" may react to such backlash by feeling "invalidated...like you are back in your family of origin." Such backlash may "reactivate several core issues...such as fear of abandonment, low self-esteem...it may push you to decrease your recovery or even drop out of it." The author-seminar speaker also criticizes the media, which he accuses of presenting "an unbalanced picture in favor of the false memory advocates":

> We know that the media is composed of workers who come from the general population, probably 80 to 95% of whom are unrecovered adult children of dysfunctional families. It should come as no surprise, then that the media would show some manifestations of being dysfunctional itself, and these presentations appear to be another example of that dysfunctional behavior.

A conference held by an organization called "Believe the Children" in June of 1994 was titled "Ritual Child Abuse: Disclosures in the 80's, Backlash in the 90's." The brochure says "this conference will examine the evolution of the backlash and propose counter measures to balance the scales of justice for those who have been victimized." Workshop titles included "False prophets of the False Memory Syndrome" and "Satan, Rituals and Child Abuse-Video

Showcase." Numerous other workshops focused on "unlocking hidden strengths that can yield confidence, energy, and wisdom," "forensic play diagnosis," "therapeutic tasks for dissociators," and a survivors panel providing a chance "for survivors to describe their most inspiring and empowering moments on the healing journey." The conference began with an address about the "emergence of multi-victim, multi-perpetrator ritual child abuse allegations and the ensuing backlash movement to *discredit child victims.*"

Do not expect this psycho-fad to go quietly into the night. This searching of the "subconscious" and probing the past is not only at the heart of the false memory phenomenon and the multiple personality fad, but also at the heart of alcohol and drug rehabilitation. This is the heart and soul of the psychotherapy industry, its major theoretical underpinning and resultant practice pattern. This has come to be economically vital. Entire livelihoods, reputations, and businesses depend on the survival of the recovery industry, and sadly, all too many of these are within the Christian community.

"For the time will come when men will not put up with sound doctrine. Instead, to suit their own desires, they will gather around them a great number of teachers to say what their itching ears want to hear. They will turn their ears away from the truth and turn aside to myths" (2 Timothy 4:3,4).

"Guard what has been entrusted to your care. Turn

away from godless chatter and the opposing ideas of what is falsely called knowledge, which some have professed and in so doing have wandered from the faith" (1 Timothy 6:20).

11

Unrepentant Recovery

◆———————◆

D O YOU SEE THE PROBLEM with Roy's recovery? You are by now aware of our view. Roy needed to face that he was separated from God because of his sin. That separation was remedied at the cross, and no amount of self-actualization techniques will bridge the gap between Roy and his Creator. Roy had simply switched from a dependency on drugs and alcohol to a dependency on his support group. Even the argument that it was of benefit to Roy since he began to function in society again is difficult to defend in Scripture. Luke 11:24-26 says, "When an evil spirit comes out of a man, it goes through arid places seeking rest and does not find it. Then it says, 'I will return to the house I left.' When it arrives, it finds the house swept clean and put in order. Then it goes and takes seven other spirits more wicked than itself, and they go in and live there. And the final condition of that man is worse than the first." Roy is less likely to seek God dressed in a three-piece suit at the Medical Society meeting than in rags vomiting in the gutter.

Drunkenness is sin. There exists no rigorously obtained, replicated, respected, or truly scientific evidence to substantiate the widely held belief that it is a disease.[1] Sufficient data does not exist to allow us to assume that the tendency to become inebriated is genetic.[2]

The modern church is determined to have the benefits of the new and hold onto what is seen as the "benefits" of the old self.

In this area, the church needs to deal with the inerrancy of 1 Corinthians 6:9-11: "Do you not know that the wicked will not inherit the kingdom of God? Do not be deceived: Neither the sexually immoral nor idolaters nor adulterers nor male prostitutes nor homosexual offenders nor thieves nor the greedy nor *drunkards* nor slanderers nor swindlers will inherit the kingdom of God. And that is what some of you *were*. But you were washed, you were sanctified, you were justified in the name of the Lord Jesus Christ and by the Spirit of our God" [emphasis ours].

The Alcoholics Anonymous model causes us to reduce our Lord and Savior to a force or god on the level of all the other "higher powers." This is as unbiblical as the term "recovering alcoholic." Scripture does not speak of recovering idolaters, recovering thieves, recovering adulterers, recovering prostitutes. It does not refer at all to recovering drunkards; instead, it clearly says that is what some of you *were*. It describes those we call alcoholics and drug addicts as "slaves to sin," and then tells us we can be freed from that slavery (Romans 6:6). "For we know that our old self was crucified with him so that the body of sin might be done away with, that we should be no longer be slaves to sin—because anyone who has died has been freed from sin."

The 12-step groups follow the doctrine of the psychology gospel and are determined to grab the benefits of what Paul called "the new life in Christ" without the crucifixion of the old. Who wants that talk about being "buried with Him into death"? The modern church is determined to have the benefits of the new and hold onto what is seen as the "benefits" of the old self.

It should come as no surprise to Christians that Alcoholics Anonymous and the 12-Step Method are of no proven scientific value.[3] Regardless of claims, popular assumptions, and testimonials of friends and relatives, the best that can be said about the alcoholism recovery industry is that it has not been "interfering with the normal recovery process."[4]

For nearly 50 years, total lifelong abstinence has

been the only allowable goal in rehabilitation programs based on the theories of Alcoholics Anonymous and its 12-step method. Some brave and much-criticized researchers question this dogma. They forward the "heresy" that perhaps "controlled" or socially appropriate drinking might be the goal of some who have been called alcoholics.[5] It should be understandable to Christians that to insist on total lifelong abstinence without the washing of the Holy Spirit and the ensuing process of sanctification might only increase the likelihood of relapse into drunkenness. Insistence on such dogma might actually be conducive to a lifetime "addiction" to continuous support and ongoing recovery.[6] "Once I was alive apart from law; but when the commandment came, sin sprang to life and I died. I found that the very commandment that was intended to bring life actually brought death" (Romans 7:9-10).

Roy needed to confess his dependency on alcohol and drugs as sin, deal with his relationship to the Lord, avoid areas where he will be tempted to return to the sin, spend time daily in the Word, and seek fellowship around that Word.

Fellowship groups can be wonderful if they are biblically based. Studying the Bible with a group and sharing its truths and insights can be exhilarating. Counsel from a mature believer can be of real benefit, especially if that believer has struggled with the same sin. We are urged in Scripture to encourage one another, to warn each other, and to hold one another accountable.

In a recovery support group, everyone's task is to share their history. Eventually everyone's story begins to sound alike, and the tale must become more lurid to get attention. People's histories actually begin to change and become fluid. What was part of one's story now becomes part of another's. Without intending to, participants in these groups begin to embellish their stories.

Psychotherapists usually accept as truth what comes from the mouths of their clients. We have already established the general unreliability of memory, but a therapist is not eager to suggest that his client is lying. Who wants to offend this one who has become so dependent on you and who you hope will pay the bill when it arrives? Most therapists accept the doctrine that, for the client, perception is reality.[7] Many therapists will say: "If the patient believes it [the memory], and if believing it helps him, then it's true." Psychotherapists true to their training have a doctrinal base that allows them to say with Pilate, "What is truth? ..." (John 18:38).

As corporations begin to accept this doctrine, management tries to listen to employee complaints. If a person's perception is his reality, what happens when 200 employees have 150 different perceptions? Are they all true because they are all believed? Someone had better answer Pilate's question or anarchy will reign.

The church that accepts this doctrine is filled with attendees dependent on support groups rather than servants depending on Jesus. We're truly in the day of the therapeutic Jesus.[8] This trend is often encouraged by church growth experts. That led us to come up with a satirical look at this phenomenon. You may smile at this as absurdity, but read between the lines and examine your own church in light of it.

To: Senior Pastor, Suburban Evangelical Church
From: President, Gamaliel Consultants
   Unlimited[9]
Re: Follow-Up on Staff Retreat

Dear Pastor:

I trust all is well with you, your staff, and your growing church. Here is the feedback and strategic plan we promised you at the retreat. I received the computerized questionnaires from your members and regular attenders. I have also obtained the local demographic and socioeconomic data from the last census. So, our plan for your church is up-to-the-minute.

It amazes even me how you have grown. What was once just another Bible-preaching church has, with our planning, mushroomed into a major player on the modern church scene. You have to admit that moving the preaching to Tuesday nights and making Sunday mornings a celebration service has really turned the corner for you.

However, as became clear at the retreat, no one should be satisfied with partial success. There is much more to be done. Our in-depth analysis of attendance patterns, giving trends, local demographics, satisfaction surveys, post-service mood assessment scales, logo recognition tests, and especially the personality tests conducted on randomly selected Sunday morning celebrators, shows us that growth at your church has plateaued. However, there is good news. The same data show that the potential for more growth is phenomenal. Our analysis shows you have certain potential for megachurch status. On that basis, we at Gamaliel are convinced that you are ready for "Plan R": Recovery.

I can imagine your excitement. We all know that the Recovery movement was "over the top" and populated by a strange crowd of experts and gurus. Though critical comments are beginning to appear in the media and Recovery may be starting to fade, that shouldn't prevent a sensitive, cutting-edge church from applying the good parts of the movement. Nobody questions the incredible suffering out there—incest, child abuse, neglect, dysfunctional families, hardship, addiction, inner-child pain, co-dependency, low self-esteem, limited self-actualization—all these and more are a plague on society. The staff in your Psychotherapy Center sees it all the time.

According to our data, 96 percent of American families are dysfunctional, and they produce children desperately in need of Recovery. Hurting people are out there and will come to your church if Recovery is offered. Our studies of your church demonstrate that almost everyone attending either had or has potential problems related to childhood trauma. The few who described themselves as happy, satisfied, or free also had high denial scores.

Most of your congregation scored high on "feeling different from other people," "sometimes putting up a false front," "not always as assertive as I would like to be," and "not enjoying life to the fullest." These were so prevalent that you can see that virtually all your people are at least candidates for Recovery.

The importance of these widespread needs cannot be overstated. No one can move beyond the constraining influences of childhood trauma without Recovery.

You have at hand a surefire way to help people achieve their potential, feel good about themselves, and feel at peace. I am certain you will want to add this new ministry product line as soon as possible. It will increase attendance dramatically and allow troubled people to solve those problems that keep them from getting close to God as they envision him.

PLAN R

This is a simple, seven-step plan to establish a successful Recovery ministry product. The objectives are to increase membership, giving, and attendance through Recovery support groups.

STEP 1—ASSESSMENT

Gamaliel has already done this for you. We have scientifically determined that all of your members and everyone in your local community was once or still is a child. Since essentially all families are (or were) either dysfunctional or in denial, these people have hurting inner children who need Recovery.

STEP 2—CONVINCE LEADERSHIP

You or some other highly credible staff member will encourage and lead the staff in a thorough study of Recovery literature (22-page bibliography attached). The subject should be discussed in staff meetings with or without invited experts (12-page listing of experts attached). You should include counseling ministers in discussions. Use videos, slide shows, and personal testimonials to underscore the message. At all times, be convincing, glib, warm, caring, and admit to your own hurting inner child in need of Recovery. Be aware that those staff who question or criticize are likely in denial of their own hurting child. They will require personal attention and special therapy.

STEP 3—PLANT SMALL SEEDS

Once the leadership is on board for the Recovery movement, begin to include Recovery books, tapes, and magazines in the church library and bookshop. Place Recovery mini-articles in the bulletin and testimonial-type articles in the church newsletter. Also encourage Recovery testimonials in some services.

STEP 4—PLANT BIG SEEDS

A series of sermons will be most effective in setting the Recovery plan in motion. Start by merely including Recovery themes or illustrations in various sermons or comment on it in other settings (e.g., weddings, funerals).

You'll want to establish the following basic Recovery precepts:

1. Our present problems result from past traumatic experiences and cannot be overcome

without remembering, reliving, and working through them by sharing with others to solve them. No need to be specific as to how exactly this is done; that ceases to be a question as time passes.

2. The influences of past trauma control our future and cause us—beyond our control or responsibility—to repeat self-destructive behavior and relationships.

3. Self-esteem, self-actualization, and inner peace will neither be achieved nor available without Recovery. These things must be achieved before we can truly love God. If we don't love ourselves, how can we love God?

STEP 5—PULL THE WEEDS

Be ready to counsel those members who are convinced that the precepts of Recovery are not in the Bible. Some may say the precepts are "in conflict" with the Bible. Others will be very insistent on this and exhibit a know-it-all attitude. These are well-intentioned but misguided fundamentalists who simply don't recognize that Recovery is throughout the Bible, just in different terms. For these you'll want to:

1. Reference scientific experts. Point the doubter to writers with Ph.D.s or M.D.s who support Recovery. Offer lots of books on the subject. Avoid getting distracted on specific biblical references, particularly passages that prove to be too open to diverse interpretation or which do not take in "the whole counsel."

2. What is truth? Point out that all truth is God's truth. Note that the Bible doesn't pretend to include all truth (e.g., physics, math) and wonder with the doubter why God gave man a mind if not to discover new truth.

3. Point to success. Can all the satisfied customers be wrong? If the outcome is good, must it not be from God? Include testimonials from prominent Christians (readily available on almost any topic).

4. Question the critic's motivation. Are they imposing their views on others? Is there something about people sharing their problems that makes them uncomfortable? Are they perhaps in denial?

5. Agree to disagree. If the doubter will not come around, insist that the disagreement be kept private. Discussing it with others will be divisive. Be prepared to lose a few members.

STEP 6—GET STARTED

This is the exciting part, the setting up of the first Recovery groups. Most popular will be Recovering Alcoholics or Adult Children of Alcoholics. That will ensure maximum participation. As time passes and word gets around, other groups will easily fall into place (e.g., Adult Victims of Child Abuse, Gamblers Anonymous, Teen Children of Divorce, and our new favorite: Friends of Children of Adult Children of Alcoholic Incest Victims). Gamaliel can help you with ideas based on our analysis of your population subgroups as new people start joining the groups.

STEP 7—GET GROWING

This involves your creativity and a chance to let your light shine. Plant articles in newspapers, do radio spots, mail fliers, and do some outside public speaking. The emphasis here is on success and inclusiveness. Everyone has the kinds of problems your ministry can solve, and everyone is welcome. No turn-offs. Emphasize the opportunity for personal growth, utilizing the power of a God of your own visualization. Be ready to add staff and space for your growing church!

The day will come when church activities you have been accustomed to will be replaced by Recovering people! With our plan, your church will be on fire. Rest assured that Gamaliel Consultants Unlimited will be with you all the way. As our motto says: What is good for church growth is good for God.

12

Psychobabble

✦————✦

"**P**SYCHOTHERAPY CAN BE BROADLY DEFINED as a talking treatment in which a trained person deliberately establishes a professional relationship with a patient for the purpose of relieving symptoms."[1]

In our culture, psychotherapy practice is diverse, widespread, respected, ingrained, and assumed to be efficacious. A recent study reviewed the *ways* in which psychotherapists have tried to prove that their therapies are, in fact, beneficial and effective. It has been found that if one applies the same standards of evidence, analysis, and proof insisted upon in any other realm of science, that conclusions of benefit or efficacy of any type of psychotherapy are simply "not warranted on the basis of either the existence of or the size of statistical effects."[2] Many other scientifically rigorous researchers have reached the same conclusions.[3] The reputation of psychotherapy as efficacious and beneficial is not justified by science but is accepted on faith.

One of the reasons for this lack of proven efficacy is that there is no single style, method, or form of psychotherapy universally agreed upon, nor is there a particular brand used by most therapists. There actually exist more than 230 recognized types of psychotherapy,[4] each one used by a varying number of practitioners.

It can be stated that there are as many psychotherapies as there are psychotherapists.[5] This seemingly flippant claim is close to fact, because "even within a type of psychotherapy administered by professionals with similar backgrounds, analysis of tape recordings of sessions has revealed considerable variations in technique."[6] To speak of "a psychotherapy" is elusive because "the characteristics of the therapist, the characteristics of the patient, and the conditions under which the therapy is to be delivered" all influence and define what is going on in any specific psychotherapeutic encounter. These same things influence even whether or not it can be compared or evaluated against another psychotherapy.[7]

So, there is no such thing as one psychotherapy with one carefully prescribed method or even a "how to" manual acceptable to a large number of therapists. The definition offered at the outset of this chapter is woefully honest in its broad description of "talking treatment."

Training in psychotherapy is part of the curriculum for psychologists, psychiatrists, social workers, probation officers, school counselors, vocational counselors, personnel officers, and other professions too numerous to name. This training curriculum is not codified and can vary from rigorous to casual. Since there is no limiting definition or defined concept of psychotherapy, it is no surprise that no rigorous, common, or reproducible training method has been forthcoming even after one hundred years of sustained effort.

Most professions have accrediting organizations which authenticate the various training programs in their fields. They measure against agreed-upon, standard sets of goals, objectives, and training experiences. These are codified in manuals, and training program directors strive to comply in order to obtain approval for their program. Program approval is only an outward sign of genuine desire to train students to do the "right thing" so the profession will have a reliable, high-quality, trustworthy product to be offered by its practitioners. Examples of this abound and run the gamut from plumbers to orthopedic surgeons.

Psychotherapy does not fit this paradigm. There is no manual of training standards. There is no "right thing" to be done, and there is no similarity expected between different programs' trainees after they have graduated and begun their practice of psychotherapy.

Many of the so-called "schools of psychotherapy" were brought into being in an effort to replicate and perpetuate the practice of a certain theorist or guru like Freud, Jung, Adler, Maslow, Fromm, Erhard, Beck. Such "schools" could come into existence, flourish, and even fade from the scene only in a field where narrow definitions are lacking.

Vast numbers of Americans are involved in psychotherapy.[8] Billions of dollars are spent in the industry. Shops are filled with books, and magazines are replete with articles, produced by or in support of this industry. One can reasonably ask why there has not emerged a body of data, rigorously collected, which would define the field. Data should affirm its theories, substantiate its claims of effectiveness, and clearly point the field toward future development. With no clear definition, with no common training curriculum, and with no common method, it is obvious that data needed to answer these questions about psychotherapy has not been forthcoming. Does simply talking with patients produce real changes? To even ask this is to be viewed by the profession as "not sensible."[9]

———————◆———————

> *Psychotherapy as a body of theory may appear coherent, plausible, sensible, and explanatory, but it never moves beyond the subjective into the realm of objective truth.*

The more fundamental explanation for the lack of hard data on psychotherapy is that the underlying foundational theses (the pillars upon which the industry rests) are decidedly not amenable to scientific examination. The pillars are not scientific.

Karl Popper, a Nobel laureate and internationally respected philosopher of science, observed decades ago that psychoanalysis and its derivatives are decidedly pseudoscientific. They lie in the same realm as astrology or Marxism, definitely separate from true science such as Einsteinian Relativity. This is because they can make no specific predictions that can be experimentally tested so as to be proven true or false.[10]

For a truthful explanation of what can be observed in man or his environment, falsifiability is essential. A true scientist will test his theories for accuracy. The real test is to devise an experiment which could prove the theory false. Einstein's theory of Relativity rang true under repeated observation. However, only when it was possible many years later to set up an experiment that would have proven the theory wrong—if it were wrong—was it finally confirmed as truth.

Psychotherapy as a body of theory may appear coherent, plausible, sensible, and explanatory, but it never moves beyond the subjective into the realm of objective truth.

The theories and practices or "talking treatment," no matter what its form, no matter what school or guru devised it, will always have as its ultimate foundation the "discoveries" of Freud late in the last century. Reducing his contributions to their most elemental, one can discern the basic underlying concepts, the pillars, of all psychotherapy practiced today:

1. Psychic determinism
2. Original innocence
3. Insight
4. Therapeutic relationship
5. Self-cure

Freud was a neurologist and, as well, a self-styled intellectual who was a keen observer of the human condition. Today he would be in a laboratory trying to observe and measure what then only his eyes and ears could record. He used those faculties, as well as his intellect and world view, to observe and try to understand the behaviors and utterances of his patients. Using his own creativity and hydraulics (the newest science of the day), he elaborated an ever more complex network of metaphors to explain what he saw and heard.

His most fundamental metaphor was that of the influence of the "unconscious" or what he called Psychic Determinism. He devised the concept of a vast world of mental activity "deep" in the mind, containing the sum total of all our cognizant experiences from birth (and as used more recently, even before birth).

To Freud, this repository powerfully and dynamically exerted its own influence on the day-to-day real-life experience of every man. He surmised that this effect manifested itself obviously as memories, but also as seemingly unexplainable thoughts, feelings, and behaviors like "slips of the tongue" and other bothersome symptoms. Freud's concept of this powerful unconscious puts man at the mercy of his past as it has been recorded and stored—according to his theory—in a realm beyond our awareness or control.

An important feature of Freud's "logic" is revealed here. His hydraulic concept of the unconscious would predict the occasional breakthrough to the surface (consciousness) of thoughts or feelings otherwise contained (repressed) in the unconscious mind. This breaking through would manifest itself in a variety of ways, according to Freud, often as a strange utterance or what have become known as Freudian slips. It is important to note that because "slips of the tongue" occur, this "proved" to Freud his theory of their origin in the unconscious. This peculiar circular logic lies at the heart of many pseudoscientific fields, such as astrology and Darwinian evolution.

Freud understood man's unconscious to be filled with all sorts of unacceptable impulses or drives which had to be contained (repressed) or somehow transformed into acceptable (neutralized) or good (sublimated) behavior. He saw man born free of evil impulses or desires, innocent, and a "clean slate." He therefore conceptualized man's problems of living (neuroses) as resulting from imperfect rearing, adverse environmental experiences having been stored in the unconscious. His theory presumes that if our rearing experiences would have been ideal, we would be ideal.

To Freud, we *are* what was done to us. We are dysfunctional (neurotic) only because of bad influences external to ourselves. This concept of Original Innocence—pure until deviated, good until polluted—is fundamental to "talking treatment."

Following upon these metaphors, Freud postulated that one could come to know, understand, and control this boiling cauldron of dynamic influences either by oneself or with a therapist as helper. By knowing and controlling (insight), one could shed the unhealthy outcroppings (neurotic symptoms) of the unconscious and bring oneself to peace. Using insight, one could remove or neutralize bad past experiences and replace them with newer healthier experiences.

The goal of psychotherapy became deep, thorough self-understanding and self-control. This could supposedly be achieved with the help of a trained professional.

Freud's theory included the assumption that one's own conscious, or the conscious of a helper, could come to know deeply and understand the unconscious of the troubled patient, and thereby change the content and influence of that unconscious. Required to do this, however, was expertise, training, special (secret) knowledge, and a "therapeutic relationship." Thus developed the almost-mythical importance of the patient-therapist relationship with all its attendant issues, which Freud himself introduced (and which have been elaborated since). Secrecy, confidentiality, suspension of the usual discriminatory faculties, re-living past experiences, and the creation of new experiences all have developed from this. The submissive, trusting patient opens himself to the caring, idealized, expertly trained therapist; then, supposedly using his own insight guided by the therapist and his own growing self-knowledge, the patient cures himself.

At the turn of the century in a world lacking any real scientific method to observe the mind, and in a world searching for answers that would bypass God's Word, Freud's metaphors swept society like a brushfire. Their apparent plausibility, their claimed efficacy, their "certainty" or their "science" quelled all doubt. Thus arose the "pseudoscience of psychoanalysis," as Karl Popper so rightfully coined it.[11]

This popular, widely accepted pseudoscience, the invention of an atheistic Viennese neurologist, has spawned every form of "talking treatment" we have today. The 250-plus therapies surviving today, despite their divergent styles and claims, rest on Freud's fundamental metaphors. The entire psychotherapeutic industry is built on these complex, fascinating ideas, which by their very nature are outside the realm of science.

Knowing this, the critical evaluation of psychotherapy is simple for the Christian. We are not born innocent and pure. The source of our trouble is not an adverse economy, poor bonding, or a hurting inner child. We are not powerless over an "unconscious" beyond our responsibility or control. The mind of man is a supernatural entity created in the image of God and never to be fully understood in this life (Jeremiah 17:9). Man cannot perfect or heal himself by himself, nor can he by using secret knowledge or a therapist-helper. Man's efforts in that direction are offensive to God (Galatians 3:3), and reliance on such false teaching is fatal to our ultimate purpose to glorify God and to enjoy Him forever.

The pillars of the psychotherapy industry are neither testable hypotheses nor proven laws of science. They are doctrines of a false religion, a false gospel.

13

A False Gospel

◆————————◆

ARE WE DEALING WITH A MINOR VARIATION in theology when we integrate psychology and Christianity? Many say it is simply expressing the same faith in a different way, that traditionalists are unable to accept expressing the faith in terms relevant to our culture.

Is that all it is? Merely the same gospel expressed in different forms?

By now you know that we say without hesitation: NO! Most fundamental is the difference between the truth of God as revealed in Scripture and the so-called truths of psychology. It is the difference between truth and falsehood, and thus, the difference between life and death. The Bible never takes doctrinal error lightly. "If anyone is preaching to you a gospel other than what you accepted, let him be eternally condemned" (from Galatians 1:8-9, authors' paraphrase).

...Do not listen to what the prophets are prophesying to you; they fill you with false hopes. They speak visions from their own minds, not from the mouth of the LORD. They keep saying to those who despise me, "The LORD says: You will have peace." And to all who follow the stubbornness of their hearts, they say, "No harm will come to you." But which of them has stood in the council of the LORD to see or to hear his word? Who has listened and heard his word?...I did not send these prophets, yet they have run with their message; I did not speak to them, yet they have prophesied. But if they had stood in my council, they would have proclaimed my words to my people and would have turned them from their evil ways and from their evil deeds. "Am I only a God nearby," declares the LORD, "and not a God far away? Can anyone hide in secret places so that I cannot see him?" declares the LORD. "Do I not fill heaven and earth?" (Jeremiah 23:16-24).

Psychology is a false gospel. Its teachers are nothing less than false prophets. They fill people with false hope and lead them to false peace. They fail to point people to their "evil deeds" and instead point them to "a God nearby" to be used for their own purposes. They do not point to the "God far away who fills heaven and earth." The God nearby and far away as described in Scriptures is clearly not the god of the psychological teachers.

He tends his flock like a shepherd, gathers the lambs in his arms, and carries them close to his heart, gently leading those that are with young. He has measured the waters in the hollow of his hand, and with the breadth of his hand marked off the heavens; he has held the dust of the earth in a basket, and weighed the mountains on the scales and the hills in a balance. Who has understood the Spirit of the Lord or instructed him as his counselor? Whom did the Lord consult to enlighten him, and who taught him the right way? Who was it that taught him knowledge or showed him the path of understanding? (from Isaiah 40, authors' paraphrase).

The true gospel delivered to us from Christ via the apostles is God-centered good news. The gospel delivered to us from psychology is man-centered and appeals to the flesh, our carnal being. It is a false gospel because of its false view of sin. The Bible is clear in its teaching of original sin:

"Surely I was sinful at birth, from the time my mother conceived me" (Psalm 51:5).

"Even from birth, the wicked go astray; from the womb they are wayward and speak lies" (Psalm 58:3).

"... Every inclination of his heart is evil from childhood" (Genesis 8:21).

"All of us have become like one who is unclean, and all our righteous acts are like filthy rags; we all shrivel up like a leaf, and like the wind our sins sweep us away" (Isaiah 64:6).

"...Jews and Gentiles alike are all under sin. As it is written there is no one righteous, not even one" (Romans 3:9-10).

———————————— ♦ ————————————

We feel the painful effects of the sins of others; but to imply that we sin because of this is contradictory to the message of Scripture.

The Bible says that each of us inevitably sins and that we do so by choice; this tendency is in our very nature, having been inherited from Adam. It is impossible to argue otherwise from Scripture. Psychology teaches that we sin because of what someone else has done to us—our parents, our spouse, our ancestors. There is no question, and it is certainly not unbiblical to say, that we feel the painful effects of the sins of others; but to imply that we sin because of this is contradictory to the message of Scripture. Not one verse indicates that our sin is produced by anyone other than ourselves. Ezekiel 18 is especially clear on this, as blaming parents apparently was one of the excuses Judah used in refusing to accept the Babylonian captivity as God's judgment.

God explains throughout Ezekiel 18 why blaming the parents is unacceptable to Him. He states in no uncertain terms that "the soul who sins is the one who will die. I take no pleasure in the death of anyone.

Repent and live!" Our need today is the same as was the need of the people of Judah: to recognize who God is, and thus to see that we stand condemned, regardless of what others have done to us. Only then can the real gospel come to us as good news; otherwise, it comes as one more technique to make us feel better. We must recognize the need for atonement, for God says clearly that without that atonement, we will die.

Once the church accepts the psychological gospel that we sin not because of who we are and what we do, but rather because of what others have done to us, then a false view of salvation and sanctification must follow. God tells us that salvation (atonement) is available for that heir to Adam's sin who cries out to God, "...Have mercy on me, a sinner" (Luke 18:13). "We all, like sheep, have gone astray, each of us has turned to his own way; and the LORD has laid on him the iniquity of us all" (Isaiah 53:6).

This good news of a redeemer is meaningless unless we recognize that we have turned to our way and are filled with iniquity. When Nathan came to David and said, "You are the man" (1 Samuel 12:7), David did not reply, "Off with your head by the king's orders! I had no choice. I had felt-needs and my sexual addiction to contend with. If I hurt anyone, it was not by choice. As a child I was neglected, given the lowliest jobs, spending long, lonely days with just sheep—no one to talk to day after day. Who can be surprised at my dysfunction?"

Instead David, described in Scripture as a man after God's own heart, said, "I have sinned against the LORD." In Psalm 51:17, he says, "The sacrifices of God are a broken spirit; a broken and contrite heart, O God, you will not despise." Instead of placing the blame elsewhere, David sees the futility of good works canceling the sin, recognizes his guilt, confesses his sins, and asks God for cleansing. David cries out to God for mercy and forgiveness from a broken and contrite heart. We are given no record of his blaming Bathsheba, or his mother, or anyone else for his sin.

Jesus makes clear in Matthew 5 that salvation comes to those with poverty of spirit, to those who realize they do not have the spiritual resources within to come face to face with God. Any awareness of the true God should produce in us the same cry as it did in Isaiah when he saw the holiness of his Creator: "Woe to me!" I cried. "I am ruined! For I am a man of unclean lips, and I live among a people of unclean lips..." (Isaiah 6:5).

Any view of the real God should produce in us a mourning over sin similar to that of Daniel (chapter 9): "We have sinned and done wrong. We have been wicked and have rebelled; we have turned away from your commands and laws. We have not listened to your servants and prophets...we are covered with shame." It should produce in us a meekness of the sort described of Moses in Numbers 12:3 ("Now Moses was a very humble man, more humble than anyone else on the face of the earth").

True salvation will produce a hungering and thirsting after righteousness as described in Psalm 119: "How I long for your precepts! My eyes stay open through the watches of the night that I may meditate on your promises. Give me understanding according to your Word" (authors' paraphrase).

Salvation produces a humility causing us to show mercy to our enemies, as did David (2 Samuel 16:11-12) when he said of Shimei: "Let him curse me, for the LORD has told him to. It may be that the LORD will see my distress." Paul reacted to his thorn in the flesh in a similar manner, saying, "It was given me to keep me from being conceited" (from 2 Corinthians 12:7, authors' paraphrase).

Salvation of the real kind makes a peacemaker of us as it did of Joseph when his brothers stood before him "terrified at his presence." Joseph said to them, "And now, do not be distressed... because it was to save lives that God sent me ahead of you" (Genesis 45:5). Accepting that payment made at Calvary for sins clears our heads related to God's purposes and brings a trust that makes us able to leave vengeance to Him.

However, salvation will also set us at odds with the world around us. Yes, it will bring persecution. Today's "user-friendly" church seems unlikely to reach any point close to Elijah in 1 Kings 19 where "Elijah was afraid and ran for his life," telling God that he was the only one left. Sadly, neither is today's church likely to receive the comfort God gave Elijah in those circumstances.

No one will be driven out of town for teaching that our troubles have come upon us because our innocent inner child was shamed and wounded, for teaching people to mourn the sins of their parents, for teaching self-esteem and assertiveness training, for leading people to hunger and thirst for attention from others, for showing mercy and compassion in the form of group therapy and Recovery programs, for adding to Scripture and thus making followers double-minded, for teaching pantheistic views of peace, and for viewing suffering as something to be eliminated as quickly as possible by whatever technique we can find.

The church today is so permeated by the false gospel of psychology that clergy and hymnwriters of the past seem ridiculous, if not laughable. Surely no one could miss the fact that they were preaching and singing about a different faith than we are embracing today.

John Donne (1573-1631), famous for his statement "Ask not for whom the bell tolls, it tolls for thee," was an Anglican clergyman, dean of St. Paul's, and a preacher to great congregations in London. He wrote: "Affliction is a treasure and scarcely any man hath enough of it. No man hath affliction enough that is not matured and ripened by it and made fit for God by that affliction. Tribulation is a treasure in the nature of it, but it is not current money in the use of it except we get nearer and nearer our home, Heaven, by it."

In John Bunyan's *Pilgrim's Progress*, Apollyan (Satan) says that Christ's servants come to ill ends and that "He has never come yet to deliver them." Christian responds in great contrast to the teaching of the modern church: "His forbearing at present to deliver them is on purpose to try their love whether they will cleave to Him to the end; as for the ill end thou sayest they come to, that is most glorious in their account. For present deliverance, they do not much expect it, for they stay for their glory and then they shall have it when their prince comes in his glory." Apollyan responds very like the modern church: "As for me, how many times have I delivered either by power or by fraud?"

Adoniram Judson Gordon, minister in Boston in the nineteenth century, wrote of the help he gained from studying the life of David Brainerd, missionary to the American Indians: "'If you would make men think well of you, make them think well of themselves' is the maxim of Lord Chesterfield which he regarded as embodying the highest worldly wisdom. On the contrary, the preacher and witness for Christ who makes us think meanly of ourselves is the one who does the most good and ultimately wins our hearts. This is exactly the effect which the reading of Brainerd's memoirs have on one. Humiliation succeeds humiliation as we read on." Surely today's church is more in tune with Lord Chesterfield than with David Brainerd or Adoniram Judson Gordon.

The following is written of Jonathan Edwards, that New England preacher so greatly used of God in the time of revival called The First Great Awakening (*Jonathan Edwards,* Banner of Truth, p. 147):

> For Edwards, profound humiliation before God and spiritual joy belong together. A sense of sin and real praise are not opposites; the saints in glory are so much employed in praise because they are perfect in humility and have so great a sense of the infinite distance between them and God (p. 259).

Edwards believed repentance in genuine Christian experience is lifelong. "True saints have mourned for sin and still do mourn. Accordingly, those who lack 'gracious affection' (real salvation) have no reverential fear, but are familiar with God in worship. In Scripture, rejoicing is not the opposite of godly fear, but is ever joined with it."

Timothy Dwight (1752-1817), Edwards's grandson and president of Yale University, in his poem entitled "The Smooth Divine" wrote of preachers who would not speak the truth:

There smiled the smooth divine, unused
   to wound
The sinner's heart, with hell's alarming
   sound.
No terrors on his gentle tongue attend;
No grating truths the nicest ear offend.
Yet from their churches saw his brethren
   driven
Who thundered Truth and spoke the voice
   of heaven.
"Let fools," he cried, "starve on, while pru-
   dent I
Snug in my nest shall live, and snug shall
   die."

Mary Rowlandson (1635-1678) was taken captive along with three of her children in Massachusetts in 1676. One child died and Mary wandered three months with the Indians. She wrote of this in a piece entitled "The Sovereignty and Goodness of God Together With the Faithfulness of His Promises Displayed":

Before I knew what affliction means, I was ready sometimes to wish for it. Scripture would come to my mind, Hebrews 12:6: "For whom the Lord loveth, He chasteneth." But now I see the Lord has His time to scourge and chasten. Affliction I had, full measure I thought, pressed down and running over. Yet I see when God calls a person to anything and through ever so many difficulties, yet He is fully able to carry them through and make them see and say they have been gainers thereby. And I hope I can say in some measure as David did, "It is good for me that I have been afflicted," and to be quieted as Moses said in Exodus 14:13: "Stand still and see the salvation of the Lord."

Such thinking is foreign to today's church, among both leaders and laymen. Anyone who would write hymns like Isaac Watts would be labeled as having a severe problem with self-worth. Watts stood in awe at the fact that God would devote "that sacred head for such a worm as I." The modern church knows little of that awe.

Christians have for two millennia seen Psalm 22 as a prophetic description of Jesus. It describes Him: "I am a worm...scorned by men and despised." The arrogant church of the twentieth century says, "What an insult for that outdated Watts to suggest that *I* am a worm!" We change Watts's wording to "such a *one* as I" and sing on.

Even Joan Baez recorded John Newton's "Amazing Grace" as he wrote it, but much of today's church won't affirm the truth that amazing grace saved "a wretch like me." We change it to "a soul like me."

What a tragic day for mankind when the church will no longer sing with Cowper:

> The dying thief rejoiced to see
> That fountain in his day;
> And there may I, tho vile as He,
> Wash all my sins away.

What? Me, vile? What an out-of-date view of this struggling, victimized race! How primitive to suggest that being plunged beneath the blood cleanses "all my guilty stains." How much more comforting to believe that what used to be called guilt is really fear, tension, anxiety, and behavior produced by stored memories.

Charles Wesley wrote:

> My chains fell off, my heart was free;
> I rose, went forth, and followed thee.
> Amazing love, how can it be
> That thou, my God, shouldst die for me!

Do our chains ever fall off via our psychologized gospel? No, they bind us only more tightly. Hymnals used as recently as 25 years ago reveal a theology widely unacceptable to today's church. It is more than a change in musical tastes that has brought about the disappearance of old hymns from our worship services and the changes in the wording of those we have retained. The original lyrics are considered relics. How many churches in the '90s would expose their people to such a "humiliation" service?

We heard a Christian psychiatrist tell a caller on a radio talk show: "Remember that old song we used to sing in Sunday school 'Jesus, Others and You, what a wonderful way to spell JOY'? Aren't you glad we no longer are expected to sing that? Now the 'you' no longer has to come last!"

Sadly, such a weak and laughable church makes Karl Marx's famous statement appear true: "Religion is the opiate of the people." Scripture memory has become a mantra for lowering blood pressure; we try to forgive others not because God commands it, but to reduce our anxiety and depression; we sing praises not because God is worthy, but because it will make *us* feel better.

Newsweek magazine, February 17, 1992, said in its cover article on self-esteem: "Churches have discovered that low self-esteem is less off-putting than sin." In its September 14, 1992 issue it covered Christian psychotherapy on the religion page and titled it, "These Souls Are Made For Shrinking."

Christianity Today (May 18, 1992), in a cover article entitled "Franchising Hope," reviewed what it termed the Christian psychiatric industry: "In March 1907 Sigmund Freud took on God, presenting a paper in which he concluded that religion was a 'universal obsessional neurosis.' Ever after, psychiatrists have seen religion as a symptom of problems, not a source of healing. No field has been more resolutely irreligious. Today's scene though would make Freud twitch."

The author obviously feels Freud would be horrified to see Christian psychiatrists invading what *Christianity Today* calls "psychiatry's realm of final authority." In our opinion, Freud would twitch with joy as he watches what the article calls "a cadre of young, confident psychotherapists talking about reforming the church, and nobody laughs."

The real horror is that hardly anybody cries, and those few who do are termed divisive, lacking in understanding, judgmental, and behind the times. *Christianity Today* had enough insight to see that the church is being reformed, or more accurately *deformed*, beyond recognition.

Freud knew that psychology and Christianity stand in total opposition. Paul wrote, "Now brothers, I want to remind you of the gospel I preached to you, which you received and on which you have taken your stand. By this gospel you are saved, if you hold firmly to the word I preached to you. Otherwise, you have believed in vain" (1 Corinthians 15:1,2).

Everyone is making a choice whether they realize it or not. You will choose the truth that sets you free or that awful bondage described so well by Bunyan: "It came burning hot into my mind that however he flattered when he got me to his house, he would sell me for a slave."

Out of those 12 years in that dark prison cell, Bunyan wrote much that would shake the modern church to its foundation:

> There can be no divine faith without a divine revelation of the will of God. Therefore, whatever is thrust into the worship of God that is not agreeable to divine revelation cannot be done but by a human faith which faith will not profit to eternal life.

Appendix

Resources for Recovering from Recovery

◆————————◆

EVERY ONE OF US faces problems, trials, and troubles. We have only two options. Will we choose God's way or the way of man?

God's way to face problems is grounded in absolute, eternal truth. His truth is authoritative and sufficient for our problems. His way is ultimately and eternally guaranteed.

Man's way of solving problems is in opposition to God's way. Whether one asks advice from a friend, seeks counsel from a "professional," or relies on a body of man-invented theory, if it is not in concert with the Word and will of God, we will be fighting with God.

The wisdom of man is relative, situational, and ever-changing. It is prone to error and cannot be trusted. What is upheld today will be decried tomorrow. We worship science because we think it should be able to give us absolute truth. We are shaken in that faith when the latest "discovery" destroys the previous one. Science, it turns out, is capable of inventing "truth" that is not God's truth after all. What might seem insight or "truth" from our past can as well be a monstrous lie.

God's way rests on the truth and promises of Scripture, employs the power of the Holy Spirit, and affords us the opportunity of help from other believers. Man's way rests on his own wisdom and traditions. Self-worship, one new technique after another, comfort and peace seen as essential, forgiveness so misunderstood as to result only in resentment, fads and fiascos, victimization and "disease" as opposed to personal responsibility, worship of science and creation versus the Creator, a clamoring for the transcendent or spiritual no matter how bizarre—these are the fruit of the false gospel of man and his psychology. These are the fruit of man and his determination to run from God.

Will you join us in sending a clarion call to the church? Make a commitment to a biblical approach to sin, atonement, and salvation and stand against the false gospel of the so-called Recovery movement. We are not in any way opposed to people seeking help and counsel. What we long for is that, if searching for such help, you will find a counselor who lovingly points you to the Scriptures and the Christ presented in that Word.

Most of the clients of Recovery therapists are women at one of two points in their lives: when their children are small and they feel trapped in the home or when their children have left the nest and they are feeling aged and useless. Men who turn to Recovery are often substance abusers and/or abusers of their wives and children.

We want to provide guidelines for choosing a counselor or staff of counselors. When you enter that office in difficulty, you are in a suggestible frame of mind. In that state of dependency, significant error can be put into your mind.

The secular counselor (or the one labeled "Christian" but who counsels from the secular base) has only the relative values of our culture to offer. He makes his decisions based on what he has read in the latest journal, the teachings of which change every month.

The counselor who believes in God will use the Bible as his guide and will expect you to do the same. He believes there is no area of our lives that stands outside the realm of that revealed Word. Our work, our families, and the way we behave as human beings are all judged by that Word; nothing is a neutral zone, free from our responsibility as Christians. A biblical counselor will point you to that absolute and eternal truth where there is no relativism or change based on evolution. He will approach your situation with certainties and with absolutes by which to measure your progress.

Here are some basics to check before committing to a counseling situation:

1. Is this a counselor who evaluates the client's relationship with the Lord? Beware those who do not consider this important. A Christian cannot counsel an unbeliever except to state truthfully that one outside Christ has no hope. "The way of the transgressor is hard," and the unbeliever must be faced with that

fact. It must be made clear that the Scripture is not a set of principles that when applied according to certain methods will open a secret kingdom of power and happiness. If a counselor temporarily soothes the conscience of an unbeliever, it is much less likely that person will see his need for a Savior.

Works done in the flesh are no better than filthy rags before the Lord (Isaiah 64:6). They won't count for eternity and they don't even last on earth. Results of these kind of deeds will not be blessed or even recognized by God.

Certainly, a counselor's first priority may be to meet a crisis: getting a client out of a dangerous, life-threatening situation. As Jay Adams says, "If you see a naked man running down the street with a meat cleaver, don't call your pastor." There are times when the police or physicians must be called. Some need hospitalization for disabling symptoms. Suicidal people may need to be restrained by police.

However, when possible, find out whether your counselor views clients as sons of Adam and daughters of Eve who need to humble themselves and admit sin in their lives.

2. Does your counselor focus on what you are actually doing, without searching for the "whys and wherefores" and someone to blame? To find help you must come to understand that before God you are without excuse. Some people *are* victims; they have been suffering at the hands of others. They need help, but even they must face their responsibility before a holy God. If your counselor explains you and your doings on the basis of some socially contrived relativistic theory, look elsewhere for help.

3. Ask the counselor to explain the theory behind his counsel. You want to hear that his authority is Scripture.

4. Ask if he sees Scripture as sufficient for every problem. You want to hear an unequivocal answer. Of course disabling symptoms may need medical treatment, even hospitalization, but not even the practice of medicine is outside the guidance of Scripture.

5. Ask how he views all truth being God's truth. Make sure your counselor does not see talking-psychology as truth. Make sure he knows the difference between man's invented "truth" and man's discovery of God's truth which will never contradict Scripture.

6. Does he believe talking-psychology is science? You know by now that the answer should be, "Absolutely not."

7. Does he integrate psychological theory with Scripture? If so, go elsewhere.

Resources that may be of help to you:

Recommended Reading

Adams, Jay E., *The Biblical View of Self-Esteem, Self-Love, and Self-Image*, Eugene, Oregon: Harvest House Publishers, 1986.

_____ *Christian Living in the Home*, Phillipsburg, New Jersey: Presbyterian & Reformed, 1972.

_____ *Competent to Counsel*, U.S.A.: Presbyterian & Reformed, 1970 (Reprinted by Zondervan).

_____ *From Forgiven to Forgiving: Discover the Path to Biblical Forgiveness*, U.S.A.: Victor Books (Scripture Press), 1989 (Reprinted by Calvary Press, Amityville, New York, 1994).

Bobgan, Deidre, *Lord of the Dance*, Eugene, Oregon: Harvest House, 1987.

Bobgan, Martin and Deidre, *The Four Temperaments, Astrology, and Personality Testing*, Santa Barbara, California: EastGate, 1992.

_____ *How to Counsel from Scripture*, Chicago: Moody Press, 1985.

_____ *Hypnosis and the Christian*, Minneapolis: Bethany House, 1984.

_____ *Prophets of Psychoheresy I and II*, Santa Barbara, California: EastGate, 1989.

_____ *Psychoheresy: The Psychological Seduction of Christianity*, Santa Barbara, California: EastGate, 1987.

_____ *12 Steps to Destruction: Codependency Recovery Heresies*, Santa Barbara, California: EastGate, 1991.

Horton, Michael, ed., *Power Religion: The Selling Out of the Evangelical Church*, Chicago: Moody Press, 1992.

MacArthur, John, *Our Sufficiency in Christ*, Dallas, Texas: Word, 1991.

Ganz, Richard, *Psychobabble: The Failure of Modern Psychology and the Biblical Alternative*, Wheaton, Illinois: Crossway Books, 1993.

Owen, Jim, *Christian Psychology's War on God's Word: The Victimization of the Believer*, Santa Barbara, California: EastGate, 1993.

Playfair, William, with George Bryson, *The Useful Lie*, Wheaton, Illinois: Crossway Books, 1991.

Sande, Ken, *The Peacemaker: A Biblical Guide to Resolving Personal Conflict*, Grand Rapids, Michigan: Baker, 1991.

Matzat, Don, *Christ-Esteem*, Eugene, Oregon: Harvest House, 1973.

Hunt, Dave, *Beyond Seduction*, Eugene, Oregon: Harvest House, 1987.

Hunt, Dave and McMahon, T.A., *The New Spirituality*, Eugene, Oregon: Harvest House, 1988.

Vitz, Paul C., *Psychology As Religion, the Cult of Self Worship*, Grand Rapids, Michigan: Eerdmans, 1977.

Brownback, Paul, *The Danger of Self Love*, Chicago: Moody Press, 1982.

Kilpatrick, William Kirk, *Psychological Seduction*, Nashville, Tennessee: Thomas Nelson, 1983.

Ice, Thomas and Dean, Robert, *A Holy Rebellion*, Eugene, Oregon: Harvest House, 1990.

Lewis, C.S., *The Abolition of Man*, New York: Macmillan, 1947.

Wells, David F., *No Place for Truth or Whatever Happened to Evangelical Theology?*, Grand Rapids, Michigan: Eerdmans, 1993.

Bulkley, Ed, *Why Christians Can't Trust Psychology*, Eugene, Oregon: Harvest House, 1993.

Broger, John C., *Self-Confrontation*, Rancho Mirage, California: Biblical Counseling Foundation, 1990.

Conyers, A.J., *The Eclipse of Heaven, Rediscovering the Hope of a World Beyond*, Downers Grove, Illinois: InterVarsity Press, 1992.

Valuable Newsletters

The Berean Call, P.O. Box 7019, Bend, Oregon 97708-7019

Psychoheresy Awareness Letter, 4137 Primavera Road, Santa Barbara, California 93110

Resource Groups

National Association of Nouthetic Counselors
5526 State Road 26 East
Lafayette, IN 47905

Christian Counseling and Education Foundation West
(offers conferences for medical doctors and biblical counseling)
3495 College Avenue
San Diego, CA 92115

Biblical Counseling Foundation
P.O. Box 925
Rancho Mirage, CA 92270
(619) 773-2667

Christian Counseling and Education Foundation
1790 E. Willow Grove Avenue
Laverock, PA 19118

L.I.F.E. Fellowship
4801 W. 115th Avenue
Westminster, CO 80020
(303) 451-LIFE

Biblical Counseling Center
3233 N. Arlington Hts. Rd.
Arlington Hts., IL 60004
(708) 398-7193

Biblical Counseling Center
1021 South Burke
Visalia, CA 93292
(209) 635-1150

Notes

Chapter 3—The Problem with Jennie—Part Two

1. J. Briere, M. Runtz, "Past Sexual Abuse Trauma: Data and Implications for Clinical Practice," *Journal of Interpersonal Violence*, Vol. 12, No. 4 (1987), pp. 367-379.

   These authors list as "trauma effects" the following: insomnia, restless sleep, nightmares, loneliness, decreased sex drive, lethargy, sadness, spacing out, anxiety attacks, uncontrollable crying, trouble controlling temper, dizziness, fainting, desire to hurt self, desire to hurt others, sexual problems, fear of men, fear of women, frequent hand washing, derealization, out-of-body experiences, chronic muscle tension, current use or abuse of psychoactive medication, history of psychiatric hospitalization, history of suicide attempts, revictimization as an adult, history of rape, drug, and alcohol addiction. Such lists are like horoscopes, so general and inclusive that most people, if so motivated, can see personal application. This phenomenon sets the stage for widespread overapplication and erroneous diagnosis.

2. Sigmund Freud, *Remembering, Repeating, and Working Through*, Standard Edition, Vol. 12 (London: Hogarth Press and the Institute of Psychoanalysis, 1914), pp. 145-155.

3. H. Muslin, "The Role of Transference in the Wolf Man Case," *J. Amer. Acad. Psychoanalysis*, 19(2) (1991), pp. 294-306.

4. Sigmund Freud, *Remembering*, p. 147.

5. D. Rieff, "Victims All?" *Harper's Magazine* (October 1991), pp. 49-56.

6. J.C. Wilson, M.E. Pipe, "The effects of cues on young children's recall of real events," *New Zealand Journal of Psychology*, Vol. 18 (1989), pp. 65-76.

7. C.A. Courtois, *Healing the Incest Wound* (New York: Norton, 1988).

8. K. Claridge, "Reconstructing memories of abuse: a theory based approach," *Psychotherapy*, Vol. 29, No. 2 (1992), pp. 243-251.

9. Ibid.

10. M. Reiser, *Handbook of Investigative Hypnosis* (Los Angeles: Law Enforcement Hypnosis Institute, 1980).

11. M. Barnes, "Hypnosis on Trial," BBC television program (London, England, 1982).

12. B. Diamond, *California Law Review* (1980), 68:313.

13. D.J. Carter, *Washington University Law Quarterly* (1982), 60:1059.

14. C. Perry, J. Laurence, *Canadian Psychology*, Vol. 24 (1983), pp. 155ff.

15. J. Laurence, C. Perry, "Hypnotically created memory among highly hypnotizable subjects," *Science*, Vol. 222 (November 1983), pp. 523-524.

16. S. Wolkind, E. Coleman, "Adult psychiatric disorder and childhood experiences," *British Journal of Psychiatry*, Vol. 143 (1983), pp. 188-191.

17. C. Brewin, "Psychopathology and early experience," *Psychological Bulletin*, Vol. 113, No. 1 (1993), pp. 82-98.

18. J. Krass, "Hypnotic memory and confidence reporting," *Applied Cognitive Psychology*, Vol. 3, No. 1 (1989), pp. 35-51.

19. E. Loftus, K. Ketcham, *Witness for the Defense* (New York: St. Martin's Press, 1991).

20. A. Barnier, K. McConkey, "Reports of real and false memories," *Journal of Abnormal Psychology*, Vol. 100, No. 3 (1991), pp. 521-527.

21. P. Sheehan, et al., "Pseudomemory effects over time in the hypnotic setting," *Journal of Abnormal Psychology*, Vol. 1, No. 1 (1991), pp. 39-44.

22. P. Sheehan, et al., "Influence of rapport on hypnotically induced pseudomemory," *Journal of Abnormal Psychology*, Vol. 101, No. 4 (1992), pp. 690-700.

23. M. Persinger, "Neuropsychological profiles of adults who report sudden remembering," *Perceptual and Motor Skills*, Vol. 75, No. 1 (1992), pp. 259-266.

24. Sigmund Freud, letter of September 21, 1897, *The Origins of Psychoanalysis* (New York: Basic Books, 1954).

25. Sigmund Freud, *From the History of an Infantile Neurosis*, Standard Edition, Vol. 17 (London: Hogarth Press and the Institute of Psychoanalysis, 1918).

26. G.S. Ellenson, "Disturbances of perception in adult female incest survivors," *Social Casework*, Vol. 67, No. 3 (1986), pp. 149-159.

27. H. Merskey, "The manufacture of personalities," *British Journal of Psychiatry*, Vol. 160 (1992), pp. 327-340.

Chapter 5—The Healing of Memories

1. "Healing the Child Within" in "Regarding Women" (Evanston, IL: Center for Women's Health, St. Francis Hospital, Fall 1992).

2. B. Graham, "Unlock the secrets of your past," *Redbook Magazine* (January 1993), pp. 84-90.

3. Ibid.

4. Ibid.

5. Ibid.

6. L. Daly, J. Pacifico, "Opening the doors to the past: decade delayed disclosure of memories of years gone by," *The Champion* (December 1991), pp. 43-47.

7. Sigmund Freud, *Remembering, Repeating and Working Through*, Standard Edition, Vol. 12 (London: Hogarth Press and the Institute of Psychoanalysis, 1914), pp. 145-155.

Chapter 7—Pastor Bill's Multiple Lives

1. John Horgan, "What if they don't have radios?" *Scientific American* (February 1993), p. 20.

2. F.W. Putnam, *Diagnosis and Treatment of Multiple Personality Disorders* (New York: Guilford Press, 1989).

3. R. Lowenstein, "Multiple personality disorder: a continuing challenge," *The Sheppard Pratt Psychiatric Review*, Vol. 2, No. 6 (1989).

4. R.P. Kluft, "The dissociative disorders," *The American Psychiatric Press Textbook of Psychiatry* (Washington, DC: American Psychiatric Press, 1988).

5. D. Russel, "Incidence and prevalence of intrafamilial and extrafamilial sexual abuse of female children," *Child Abuse and Neglect*, Vol. 7 (1983), pp. 133-146.

6. C.A. Ross, et al., "Structured interview data on 102 cases of multiple personality disorder from four centers," *American Journal of Psychiatry*, Vol. 147 (1990), pp. 596-601.

7. S. Boon, N. Draijer, "Multiple personality disorder in the Netherlands," *American Journal of Psychiatry*, Vol. 150, No. 3 (1993), pp. 489ff.

8. Y. Takahishi, "Is multiple personality disorder really rare in Japan?" *Dissociation*, Vol. 3 (1990), pp. 57-59.

9. R. Allison, T. Schwarz, *Minds in Many Pieces* (New York: Rawson Wade, 1980).

10. H. Merskey, "The manufacture of personalities," *British Journal of Psychiatry*, Vol. 160 (1992), pp. 327-340.

11. M.A. Simpson, "Multiple personality disorder," *British Journal of Psychiatry*, Vol. 155 (1989), pp. 565ff.

12. R. Aldridge-Morris, *Multiple Personality: An Exercise in Deception* (London, England: Lawrence Erlbaum Associates, 1989).

13. S.L. Mitchill, "A double consciousness, or a duality of person in the same individual," *Medical Repository* (New Series), Vol. 3 (1816), pp. 185-186.

14. E.E. Azam, "Amnesie periodique, ou doublemente de la vie," *Revue Scientifique*, 2me Serie, X (1876), pp. 481-489.

15. M. Prince, *The Dissociation of a Personality*, Second Edition (London, England: Longman Green, 1908).

16. C.H. Thigpen, H.M. Cleckley, *The Three Faces of Eve* (New York: McGraw-Hill, 1957).

17. A. Daniels, *The Daily Telegraph* (November 13, 1990), p. 17.

18. Merskey, "The manufacture."

19. F. Frankel, "Hypnotizability and dissociation," *American Journal of Psychiatry*, Vol. 147 (1990), pp. 7ff.

Chapter 9—Lovers of Self

1. A.A. Dallimore, *George Whitefield* (Southhampton, England: Camelot Press, 1980).

2. J. Bunyan, *The Pilgrim's Progress* (Westwood, NJ: Barbour and Company, 1985).

Chapter 11—Unrepentant Recovery

1. B. Rush, "An inquiry into the effects of ardent spirits" in *A New Deal in Liquor, a Plea for Dilution*, Y.A. Henderson, editor (New York: Doubleday, 1934).

   E.M. Jellinek, *The Disease Concept of Alcoholism* (New Haven: Yale University Press, n.d.).

   H. Fingarette, *Heavy Drinking: The Myth of Alcoholism as a Disease* (Berkeley, CA: University of California Press, 1988).

2. R.W. Pickens, et al., "Heterogeneity in the inheritance of alcoholism," *Archives of General Psychiatry*, Vol. 48 (1991), pp. 19-28.

   C. Holden, "Probing the complex genetics of alcoholism," *Science*, Vol. 251, No. 11 (January 1991), pp. 163-164.

3. F. Baekeland, et al., "Methods for the treatment of chronic alcoholism: a critical appraisal" in *Research Advances in Alcohol and Drug Problems*, Vol. 2 (1975).

   Fingarette, *Heavy Drinking*.

   S. Peele, *Diseasing of America: Addiction Treatment Out of Control* (Lexington, MA: D.C. Heath Company, 1989).

4. G. Vailaant, *The Natural History of Alcoholism* (Cambridge, MA: Harvard University Press, 1983).

5. D. Armor, J.M. Polich, H.B. Stambul, *Alcoholism and Treatment* (Santa Monica, CA: The Rand Corporation, 1976).

   N. Heather, I. Robertson, *Controlled Drinking* (London, England: Methuen, 1981).

6. Wm. Playfair, *The Useful Lie* (Wheaton, IL: Crossway Books, 1991).

7. K. Claridge, "Reconstructing memories of abuse: a theory based approach," *Psychotherapy*, Vol. 29, No. 2 (1992), pp. 243-251.

8. D.F. Wells, *No Place for Truth or Whatever Happened to Evangelical Theology* (Grand Rapids, MI: Eerdmans, 1993).

9. Acts 5:34-35,38-39: "But a Pharisee named Gamaliel...addressed them: '...if their purpose or activity is of human origin, it will fail. But if it is from God, you will not be able to stop these men; you will only find yourselves fighting against God.'"

Chapter 12—Psychobabble

1. H. Kaplan, B. Sadock, *Comprehensive Textbook of Psychiatry*, Fifth Edition (Baltimore, MD: Williams & Wilkins, 1989), p. 1568.

2. N.S. Jacobson, P. Traux, "Clinical significance: a statistical approach to defining meaningful change in psychotherapy research," *Journal of Consulting and Clinical Psychology*, Vol. 59, No. 1 (1991), pp. 12-19.

   Other competent researchers into this subject have identified the problems with past and traditional studies of psychotherapy which claimed to prove that it was efficacious or beneficial. Some are listed below:

   D.H. Barlow, "On the relation of clinical research to clinical practice: current issues, new direction," *Journal of Consulting and Clinical Psychology*, Vol. 49 (1981), pp. 147-155.

   S. L. Garfield, "Evaluating the psychotherapies," *Behaviors Therapies*, Vol. 12 (1981), pp. 295-307.

   N.S. Jacobson, et al., "Psychotherapy outcome research: methods for reporting variability and evaluating clinical significance," *Behavior Therapy*, Vol. 15 (1984), pp. 336-352.

   P.C. Kendall, J.D. Norton-Ford, "Therapy outcome research methods" in *Handbook of Research Methods in Clinical Psychology* (New York: Wiley, 1982), pp. 429-460.

   M.L. Smith, G.V. Glass, T.I. Miller, *The Benefits of Psychotherapy* (Baltimore, MD: Johns Hopkins Press, 1980).

3. A.E. Kazdin, "Effectiveness of psychotherapy with children and adolescents," *Journal of Consulting and Clinical Psychology*, Vol. 59, No. 6 (1991), pp. 785-798.

4. C.P. O'Brien, G.E. Woody, "Evaluation of psychotherapy" in *Comprehensive Textbook of Psychiatry*, Fifth Edition, Kaplan

and Sadock, editors (Baltimore, MD: Williams & Wilkins, 1988).

5. Ibid.

6. A.E. Kazdin, *Child Psychotherapy: Developing and Identifying Effective Treatments* (Elmsford, NY: Pergamon Press, 1988).

7. M. Weisman, J. Meyers, P. Harding, "Psychiatric disorders in a U.S. urban community," *American Journal of Psychiatry*, Vol. 135 (1978), pp. 459-467.

8. Kazdin, *Child Psychotherapy*.

9. Ibid.

10. J. Horgan, "The intellectual warrior," *Scientific American* (November 1992), pp. 38-44.

11. Ibid.